Project Monitoring and Evaluation in Agriculture

A Joint Study

The World Bank

International Fund
for Agricultural
Development

Food and Agriculture
Organization of the
United Nations

This book is the first in a series on the monitoring and evaluation of agriculture projects. The series will include a companion volume, *The Collection, Analysis, and Use of Monitoring and Evaluation Data*, as well as brief technical notes.

Project Monitoring and Evaluation in Agriculture

Dennis J. Casley and Krishna Kumar

Ram C. Malhotra, editor of the series ·

Published for The World Bank
The Johns Hopkins University Press
Baltimore and London

The Johns Hopkins University Press
Baltimore, Maryland 21211, U.S.A.

The findings, interpretations, and conclusions
expressed in this study are the results of research
supported by the World Bank, but they are entirely
those of the authors and should not be attributed
in any manner to the World Bank, to its affiliated
organizations, to members of its Board of
Executive Directors or the countries they represent;
to the International Fund for Agricultural
Development; or to the Food and Agriculture Organization
of the United Nations.

First printing October 1987

Library of Congress Cataloging-in-Publication Data

Casley, D. J.
    Project monitoring and evaluation in agriculture.

    "Published for the World Bank."
    "A joint study: the World Bank, International Fund
for Agricultural Development, Food and Agriculture
Organization of the United Nations"—P.
    Bibliography: p.
    Includes index.
    1. Agricultural development projects—Management.
2. Agricultural development projects—Evaluation.
I. Kumar, Krishna, 1940-   . II. International Bank
for Reconstruction and Development. III. International
Fund for Agricultural Development. IV. Food and
Agriculture Organization of the United Nations.
V. Title.
HD1415.C335   1987   351.82'33   87-22632
ISBN 0-8018-3615-8
ISBN 0-8018-3616-6 (pbk.)

Cover photograph: Winnowing grain in Chad. By A. Girod.
Courtesy Food and Agriculture Organization
of the United Nations.

Contents

The Environment   150
The Role of National Survey Agencies   153

Examples

Preface

BECAUSE OF THE NEED TO MONITOR the implementation of projects and evaluate their achievements, these activities are now a routine part of project appraisal. Monitoring and evaluation components in agriculture projects have been provided since the emphasis on rural development and poverty alleviation in the mid-1970s. But many of these early efforts proved unsatisfactory.

In the early 1980s several agencies recognized the problems in formulating effective monitoring and evaluation systems and issued guidelines for project design staff and handbooks for practitioners; the World Bank, the International Fund for Agricultural Development (IFAD), and the Food and Agriculture Organization of the United Nations (FAO) were among these. Unfortunately, there was no agreement on the usage of such technical words as monitoring, evaluation, input, output, and impact or on distinctions between the monitoring and evaluation functions and the appropriate priority for each.

A great deal of further evidence has been garnered since 1980, and discussions on the appropriate concepts and recommended methodologies have proceeded apace. Within the U.N. system these discussions have been held within the forum of the Panel on Monitoring and Evaluation set up in 1981 by the U.N. Administrative Committee on Coordination (ACC) Task Force on Rural Development. In 1984 this task force issued *Guiding Principles for the Design and Use of Monitoring and Evaluation in Rural Development Projects and Programs* (Rome: United Nations, 1984), which reflected progress toward a consensus on concepts, definitions, and methods.

Since 1980 progress has been achieved in setting up and implementing effective monitoring and evaluation systems. In a recent survey of current World Bank projects, three-quarters of the monitoring systems were rated at least adequate by World Bank staff. Even for these satisfactory systems, however, monitoring was found to be limited in scope; it covered physical and financial information but was often deficient in information on the vital linkage of the project with the intended beneficiaries. For the evaluation systems, the survey revealed that ambitions for measuring project impact in a limited span of years remain high and universal, but these ambitions are not matched by the achievements of impact studies. Most of these have failed to provide even a sound data base, let alone allow for an analysis that would meet the high expectations of the designers. In general, there is inadequate understanding of the limitations of current evaluation methodology and of the need for project designers, managers, and evaluators to adapt techniques accordingly.

The accumulating experience and the growing consensus regarding concepts and definitions led the World Bank and IFAD (agencies concerned with funding investment projects) in collaboration with the FAO to agree to produce a set of technical publications on the monitoring and evaluation of agriculture investment projects which would provide the basis for training programs at the regional and national levels. This book provides a conceptual framework. A companion volume, *The Collection, Analysis, and Use of Monitoring and Evaluation Data* (Baltimore, Md.: Johns Hopkins University Press, forthcoming), provides specific methodological guidance.

This book is based on the ACC Task Force *Guiding Principles* and builds on that structure to develop monitoring and evaluation concepts and definitions in the particular context of agriculture investment projects. Chapter 1 provides the perspective from which information systems need to be designed—the perspective of project management. This requires that due priority be placed on establishing and maintaining a management information system to monitor the project as a means of facilitating sound management decisionmaking. The components of such a system and the execution of the monitoring function are described in chapters 2 through 6.

Chapters 7 through 9 discuss project evaluation. The various types of evaluation are discussed in chapter 7, which thus illustrates how the management information system can be used and also outlines the supplementary data series that may be required. Chapter 8 discusses the methods and limitations of the most commonly featured evaluation objective, the measurement of change in crop production. Failure to appreciate these limitations has been the biggest single reason for overambitious designs that did not succeed. Finally, chapter 9 includes a discussion of particular evaluation issues in connection with certain special topics.

Examples of actual monitoring and evaluation problems are interspersed in the text to illustrate significant points. These narratives have been edited and in some cases sharpened to dramatize the point being made. A full reference is given if the source document is available. In many cases, however, the source document is restricted and only the agency name is given.

This book, together with its companion volume, largely supersedes the earlier technical publications that preceded the ACC publication. In particular, it replaces and expands upon Dennis J. Casley and Denis A. Lury, *Monitoring and Evaluation of Agriculture and Rural Development Projects* (Baltimore, Md.: Johns Hopkins University Press, 1981).

The companion book, *The Collection, Analysis, and Use of Monitoring and Evaluation Data*, consists of technical discussions of the issues connected with data collection, analysis, and presentation that experience has shown are those on which advice is most commonly sought. It will discuss qualitative interviews, participant observation, and other informal methods. The quantitative methods covered will include survey design and use, with special consideration of rural household surveys; sampling; data processing and analysis; crop production estimation; and data presentation.

It is necessary to stress what this book and its companion are not. They do not deal with monitoring and evaluation of national programs and policies. For example, monitoring the levels of poverty or evaluating the effectiveness of national agrarian reform policies each presents a different set of issues. The framework and the systems proposed here are put forward solely in the context of the monitoring and evaluation of agriculture and rural development investment projects, which are defined as interrelated and coordinated activities formulated and financed to achieve a specific set of objectives within a limited span of time and operated by an identifiable and formally responsible management team.

The volumes were written by individuals and therefore should not be taken to reflect the official views of the three institutions. In general, however, they indicate a common thrust to improve monitoring and evaluation activities. The primary intended audience comprises those in the developing world responsible for the design and implementation of monitoring and evaluation systems. Project managers may also benefit from this first volume, particularly the early chapters. I also hope that these publications will be useful to those who provide training courses in this subject and to all who are interested in the vital issue of judging the success of the development effort in rural economies.

RAM C. MALHOTRA
Director, Monitoring and Evaluation Division,
International Fund for Agricultural Development,
and Convenor-Chairman, Panel on Monitoring
and Evaluation, U.N. ACC Task Force on Rural
Development

Acknowledgments

The authors acknowledge the contributions made by many of their colleagues in the preparation of this book. In particular, the preparation of the materials for the examples, together with a contribution to chapter 9, were the work of Diana Crowley. Ronald Ng and Eric Clayton were mainly responsible for drafting chapter 3. We are grateful for the assistance of Ram Malhotra of the International Fund for Agricultural Development, whose role is acknowledged on the title page. Chandra Arulpragasam of the Food and Agriculture Organization (FAO) coordinated the FAO contribution, which included valuable comments from Françoise Petry, Monica Fong, Abdul Ayazi, and Masakatsu Kato. Valuable editorial suggestions were also received from Josette Murphy, Vinh Le-Si, Ted Rice, and Roger Slade. The contributions of all the above were substantial, but nevertheless the authors acknowledge responsibility for the overall emphasis and of course for any errors of interpretation. Finally, we express our appreciation to Michael Alloy, who processed the manuscript.

1 | Monitoring and Evaluation: A Management Perspective

MONITORING AND EVALUATION functions are presented here in the context of the planning, implementation, and completion of an agriculture or rural development project. This requires treating monitoring and evaluation as part of the process of project management and thus viewing objectives, concepts, design, and methodologies from the perspective of the project manager.

This perspective has major implications for the design and application of monitoring and evaluation systems. It emphasizes monitoring as an internal project activity and calls for diagnostic studies as part of its function of aiding management decisionmaking. It considers evaluation to be the assessment of a project's performance and impact on the target population and area. Initial assessments are relevant to project management and central authorities, but formal impact evaluation requires a time frame that may extend beyond the project's life span, so the demand for and use of such evaluation lie mainly with central agencies and funding institutions.

One of the principal causes of the failure of many monitoring and evaluation efforts has been misunderstanding at the design stage of the purpose of such efforts. Project managers often view monitoring and evaluation units as surveillance agents operating on behalf of the concerned ministries or, even worse, as agents of funding institutions. Unfortunately, in many instances such views are justified, for monitoring and evaluation activities are often confined to the surveillance of a broad development program and the conduct of impact studies. It is the purpose of this book to set out the concepts of and framework for monitoring and evaluation so as to correct such misunderstandings and avoid the consequent misapplications.

Various authors define monitoring and evaluation differently, and this leads to semantic confusion. *Guiding Principles for the Design and Use of Monitoring and Evaluation in Rural Development Projects and Programmes*[1]

1. *Guiding Principles for the Design and Use of Monitoring and Evaluation in Rural Development Projects and Programmes* (Rome: United Nations, 1984). Hereafter, *Guiding Principles.*

1

provides definitions that embrace common usage by all U.N. agencies, but we have sought to provide definitions that can be interpreted unambiguously within the specified context of agriculture investment projects.

Monitoring is a continuous assessment both of the functioning of the project activities in the context of implementation schedules and of the use of project inputs by targeted populations in the context of design expectations. It is an internal project activity, an essential part of good management practice, and therefore an integral part of day-to-day management.

Evaluation is a periodic assessment of the relevance, performance, efficiency, and impact of the project in the context of its stated objectives. It usually involves comparisons requiring information from outside the project—in time, area, or population.

The monitoring function is carried out by using the data within a management information system. Such a system includes the basic physical and financial records, the details of inputs and services provided to beneficiaries (for example, credit and extension advice) and the data obtained from surveys and other recording mechanisms designed specifically to service the monitoring function.

Evaluation will also draw on the management information system, but with a view to comparisons over time and against comparable "control" information. The full exercise of the evaluation function will require, in selective cases, supplementing the project management information system with data from impact studies that may be designed and executed outside the project management system itself.

We will elaborate on these definitions as we describe the activities that need to be carried out within the monitoring and evaluation functions. But the use of these terms needs to be clearly understood in view of differing interpretations in the extensive literature on this subject. *Guiding Principles* stresses the relationship between monitoring and evaluation while recognizing the distinctions between them. This book, reflecting further reviews of project experience, stresses the distinction between the monitoring and evaluation functions while recognizing their related features; in consequence, and consistent with *Guiding Principles*, there is no stress on the ubiquity of a monitoring and evaluation unit as such. Also, *Guiding Principles*, reflecting the common and current usage, describes the continuous assessment of the relevance, efficiency, and effectiveness of a project during implementation as "ongoing evaluation." In describing the precise components involved in monitoring and evaluation, we have preferred to label each component individually. The reader familiar with *Guiding Principles* will recognize that our individual descriptions of beneficiary contact monitoring, diagnostic studies, and internal (including midterm) evaluation together form what much of the literature, including *Guiding Principles*, refers to as ongoing evaluation. Our basic position is that certain ongoing activities undertaken for monitoring purposes feed into evaluation.

The full potential of the monitoring function can be realized only when it is seen as an integral part of the management process; conversely, it cannot succeed unless project managers accept its importance and usefulness. Good management will require, and demand, a good management information system. But such a system, however conceptually sound, cannot survive ineffective management or badly designed management structures.

The potential of evaluation will be achieved if it is clearly understood who is to use the results and for what purposes and if the practical limitations are accepted of available methodology in applied project environments.

Managing Development Projects

The crucial need for information systems becomes obvious when we look at the various generic tasks which managers of a development project have to undertake:

- Further specify the project objectives, using the original statements in appraisal documents, as a basis for preparing a detailed implementation strategy
- Develop appropriate activities and delivery systems and determine the required inputs and outputs
- Prepare realistic work plans and schedules, keeping in view the available resources and staff capabilities
- Determine the precise responsibilities of the various organizational units and their staffs
- Maintain detailed records of physical and financial performance
- Establish realistic, measurable performance indicators based on feasibility, costs, and capabilities
- Supervise the performance of individuals and organizational units
- Monitor the project environment so that it can facilitate project implementation or so that suitable adjustments can be made in ongoing or planned activities
- Provide periodic reports to the responsible central agencies and institutions.

Management personnel at various levels of the project hierarchy need timely and relevant information to undertake these tasks. The primary role of monitoring is to assist management in establishing and maintaining the required information system and to use it in a timely fashion. Monitoring encompasses the collation of recorded project data and the collection of supplementary data for the analysis and interpretation required to make decisions concerning the functioning of the project. Monitoring staff assist in the operation of a management information system in the following ways:

- Identify, in cooperation with management, the targets for project implementation and the indicators to measure progress against these targets
- Collate, summarize, and disseminate the information flowing from the various agencies and staff engaged in implementing the project
- Analyze the administrative files and records pertaining to project implementation
- Collect and analyze data from the intended beneficiaries of the project to supplement the available records and reports
- Identify problems encountered by the project and conduct diagnostic studies bearing on these problems
- Maintain in a retrievable format, the various data series over time as an aid to later evaluation
- Prepare reports that highlight the findings of the various analyses and, to the extent appropriate, present a range of logical options requiring decisions by management.

Evaluation then draws on the data base created during the monitoring process, supplementing it as necessary with data on project impact, and reviewing the combined information over an extended period to judge achievement. Of course, monitoring and evaluation functions differ from project to project depending on the type of project and its components. Broadly speaking, agriculture and rural development projects can be classified into two categories: physical delivery projects and people-centered projects.[2] The first category includes building and maintaining infrastructure and operating plants and utilities. Management systems for these are generally well understood: the professional and technical skills can be specified, and the physical tasks and targeting of these tasks are familiar to those possessing these skills, so that management needs only to motivate, control, and facilitate the work of the project staff. Moreover, because progress in implementation, monitoring of performance, and evaluation of achievement can be measured against physical output targets, monitoring and evaluation are almost automatically built into project operations.

People-centered projects, however, are more difficult to manage because of the less tangible goals and the less precisely specified means of

2. See, for example, chapter 9 of World Bank, *World Development Report 1983* (New York: Oxford University Press, 1983).

attaining these goals. Goals such as increasing the participation of beneficiaries in the project and raising the quality of life are abstract. Achievement of these goals requires changes in the behavior patterns of the people concerned; prediction of whether, in what way, and at what rate such changes will occur is so uncertain that it is difficult to specify targets for measuring implementation performance. Indeed, one of the tasks of managing people-centered projects in many cases is to give the intended beneficiaries an increased awareness of the constraints on their lives so as to stimulate demand for the services that the project has to offer.

As we move from physical delivery projects to people-centered ones, the task of internal monitoring becomes more important and more challenging. In a physical delivery project, monitoring is almost synonymous with the maintenance of records of physical and financial progress, but in people-centered projects, the routine need for physical and financial information is supplemented by a considerable requirement for data relating to linkages between the project's infrastructure and personnel and the target population.

The Monitoring Focus for the Management Information System

As indicated above, in order to implement a project, the manager needs a regular flow of information on the resources (staff, equipment, money, and so forth) deployed and deployable, the stage of preparation of infrastructure and services, the availability and supply of inputs, the contact with targeted beneficiaries and their reactions to the stimulus offered by the project, and the environment as it affects the implementation of the project. This range of required information can be divided into three main categories:

- Information pertaining to the physical delivery of the structures and services provided by the project, together with the relevant financial records
- Information pertaining to the use of the structures and services by the targeted population and the initial consequences of that use
- Information on the social, economic, or environmental reasons for any unexpected reaction by the target population that is revealed by the information about the use of the structures and services.

The monitoring function, as elaborated here, covers not only the physical and financial information but also a second category, which we term the beneficiary contact information system, as well as a third category, which we term project diagnostic studies. Any project with an active management will have some system for recording physical and financial information; chapter 3 describes the contents of such a system. But even though this information is an integral part of the monitoring process, it is often neglected or not recognized as part of a project's so-called monitoring and evaluation effort. This is because the physical and financial information is usually the responsibility of financial and procurement offices within the project, and the monitoring and evaluation functions are seen as having little or no connection with the use of such information. In other words, a large part of the monitoring is omitted. In example 1, criticism of the monitoring and evaluation component of the project was related solely to a farm survey, with no reference to the existence and sound utilization of a good management information system.

EXAMPLE 1. *Narrowly Focused Review of Monitoring*

When a country perceived the need to increase its meat and milk production, a livestock improvement project was funded to strengthen the national livestock agency, provide credit to finance the development of livestock farms, and provide extension and animal health services to help farmers manage their operations. At the project's completion, an evaluation team rated the project an overall success since the national livestock agency grew into a stronger and more effective technical organization and the credit and services succeeded in spreading modern livestock development technology throughout the country.

　Under the heading of monitoring and evaluation, however, the review was critical. The only function identified by the team as monitoring was a farm survey; other information-utilization activities were thus excluded from the review. It was noted that the livestock agency's survey had been unsuccessful in a portion of the project area, for the owners were absent at the time of the intended interview. Because of its narrowly focused approach, the evaluation team cited this problem as evidence of weak monitoring. In a later overview of monitoring and evaluation performance in a set of projects, this one was rated as "poor." However, the project management had actually developed and used a good information system and had successfully monitored project performance. Project staff were able to prepare a detailed analysis of project progress, including information on disbursements, type and location of farms financed, credit repayment rates, and dissemination of livestock farming technology.

　The physical and financial information system revealed at an early stage that the agency's farm development funds were being rapidly committed and that shortages might occur. At completion, project records showed that loans granted amounted to $151.5 million, compared with appraisal estimates of $106.1 million.[3] A national livestock development program was developed in response to these findings and served as a basis for securing additional staff

---

3. Unless noted, all dollars are U.S. dollars.

and resources. Provincial governments and the banking sector provided the needed resources.

At completion, project records enabled the staff to portray precisely the project's demand for livestock financing and its geographical pattern. It provided financing for the development of 1,589 livestock farms—515 dairy farms, 589 sheep farms, and 485 beef farms. The loan financed a greater number of dairy and sheep farms and a smaller number of beef farms than had been projected at appraisal. A total of 2,985 loan applications were received in the southern project area, and 3,223 in the northern area.

The presence of this information system, although not recognized as monitoring by the evaluation team, enabled management to complete the project successfully. Its ability to produce timely reporting on project progress made it an effective management tool and led directly to decisions that were crucial to the outcome of the project.

Source: World Bank.

Commonly, a project's monitoring and evaluation system focuses to some extent on the second component of the management information system outlined above, but it concentrates on collecting data to be used later for evaluation. Regardless of the issue of evaluation, however, the monitoring function should encompass all three categories of the management information system. Even though the recording of physical progress and the maintenance of the financial accounts may appropriately be well-defined activities of separate units, it is nevertheless necessary to draw on such records in the monitoring process.

Establishing linkages among the accumulating data is part of the monitoring function. Physical and financial information that is maintained solely for recording and audit purposes stands alone and, in that sense, is underutilized. Such data must be linked with beneficiary contact information so that the delivery of a service at a certain cost can be assessed against the market for that service. And without follow-up diagnostic studies of the unexpected reactions that monitoring reveals, monitoring cannot fulfill its fundamental purpose of improving management decisionmaking.

The monitoring function should focus on the interaction between the project activities and reactions of the target population if it is to meet the needs of management. Management attention to the mechanics of procurement, storage, and delivery of a farm input is justified only if the intended users agree that it is the right input, delivered to the right place and at the right time. Filling the stores with fertilizer two months after the planting season is a useless activity, even if the procurement was at a favorable price and the stores were built efficiently according to specifications and budget.

Monitoring is concerned with the points of contact between project and beneficiaries, where project activities encounter the population's perceptions and expectations. Individual parts of the information system have a value in their own right as records and as the basis for action by individual project staff—for example, as a reminder to order more stationery when stocks fall to a certain level. But the monitoring officer has to select the data and convert them to indicators that throw light on the implementation of the project in the context of how it is affecting the local population.

A cautionary word may be offered regarding beneficiary contact monitoring and diagnostic studies. As is emphasized throughout this book, monitoring is a tool for project managers to use in judging and influencing the progress of implementation. Managers have the responsibility for deciding the tactics for implementation within the strategy laid down in the documentation. The role of monitoring is not to put these tactics continuously under question by setting up a survey system to explore other options. Monitoring should provide managers with the information that will maximize their chance of succeeding with the chosen tactics. As problems emerge, diagnostic studies may well indicate flaws that throw into question the project strategy or implementation tactics or both, but such studies are supplements to, not substitutes for, the provision of information geared to current implementation procedures.

Monitoring and Evaluation as Distinct Functions

The argument put forward so far leads to a fundamental question. Are monitoring and evaluation such distinctly different functions, serving distinctly different users, that they should be considered independently of each other? The answer to this question, in the light of the definitions given here, is yes. Hence we disapprove of the use of the universal acronym "M&E" as it can imply that we are dealing with a single function. Monitoring and evaluation are separated by their objectives, reference periods, requirements for comparative analysis, and primary users. But having emphasized the differences, we need to enter a qualification: in spite of these distinct functions, there are common features which highlight the relationship between them. In many cases, the same data collection and analysis system will be used for both, and the indicators for monitoring may be included in the range of information required for evaluation, but they will be reviewed over a longer time span, with the use of comparative analytical techniques, and a larger group of users will be addressed. The monitoring of a project may itself reveal such significant departures from expectations that it calls for an interim, internal evaluation. This will assess the likely outcome if such experiences continue and will review the case for a major reappraisal of the assumptions and premises for the project design.

Monitoring must be integrated within the project management structure, but evaluation, with its wider horizons, is not necessarily such an integral component. Evaluation responsibilities may be located within a central unit at the national level. But both the project monitoring function and the central evaluation function must collaborate in order to use resources efficiently without losing sight of the primary purpose of the project's internal information-gathering resources—the provision of an information system designed to meet the needs of project management.

A central evaluation facility at the national level may be justified on several grounds:

- The demanding professional skills required to interpret evaluation data are either unavailable or uneconomic to provide for each project individually.
- The required data series extends from a time before a project is initiated to a period past its completion.
- It is necessary to have data from within and without the project population to achieve some form of rudimentary control comparisons.
- Evaluation techniques can be applied uniformly to a development program involving interproject comparisons.
- A measure of independence from the project facilitates objectivity in the analysis.

The collaboration between a central evaluation facility and the project's own monitoring activities can benefit both. The evaluation facility, while conducting the national evaluation of the development effort, can provide professional and survey skills for selected individual projects. Meanwhile, the monitoring resources within a project can gather much of the data for a centralized design and analytical facility for evaluation. But caution is needed. If the central facility's work program is dictated by national evaluation needs and demands data that have little relevance to a particular project, there is considerable danger that these national needs will divert the project's data collection from meeting the monitoring needs of the project management.

Example 2 outlines a case in which a central unit dominated the decisions regarding the survey design and data content of the monitoring and evaluation systems of the projects that were managed at the state level. Project management therefore gave less than wholehearted support to the data collection work and neither project nor national requirements were met.

EXAMPLE 2. Relationships between a Central and a Project Unit

A federal monitoring and evaluation agency was charged with the long-term evaluation of a national food plan. But the same agency, with its high-level skills in survey design, data collection, and analysis, was also responsible for supporting the monitoring and evaluation units in each of several large state agricultural projects. Given its broad mandate and concentration of resources, the central agency assumed a dominant role in determining the thrust of the monitoring and evaluation program in each state project, which therefore tended to focus on the data needs for evaluating the national food plan.

The agency developed a work program for project monitoring and evaluation units which included annual agronomic surveys based on probability samples of farmers designed to provide statewide aggregate estimates of crop areas and production for use at the national level. These surveys demanded considerable staff resources and field time from each project monitoring and evaluation unit. Project management, although willing to provide staff resources to carry out these surveys, increasingly felt that the work program was dominated by long-term evaluation requirements at the expense of their internal monitoring requirements, which focused on the delivery of services in certain areas within the state.

From the outset, a loosely defined administrative framework obscured the central agency's authority within the monitoring and evaluation system. For example, the project document that established the federal agency's terms of reference implied that the agency would hold a large measure of control over the project monitoring and evaluation units. The documents that established the agricultural projects, however, described the reverse situation: monitoring and evaluation activities were to be determined by project management with technical assistance from the central agency. These varying descriptions of the administrative arrangements prevented a consensus among federal and project staffs as to who should lead monitoring and evaluation activities.

Furthermore, the agency's standardized survey provided neither the flexibility nor the focus required by the multicomponent projects. For example, the broad sweep of the sampling technique used in the agronomic survey provided only state-level estimates; it did not allow for the data to be broken down to the local level. A project developing local farm service centers could not use the survey to analyze local beneficiaries' initial reactions.

The project monitoring and evaluation units seemed unable to meet project management demands for ad hoc investigations, at least in part because the central agency required them to concentrate on the survey program. Some project managers felt that the monitoring and evaluation units were more allied to this agency than to their own project. The necessarily close links between monitoring and evaluation units and the federal agency during normal management of the survey added to this suspicion.

A more equitable sharing of monitoring and evaluation resources between the central agency and project management was clearly necessary. The com-

bined resources of the central agency and the projects were substantial enough to have permitted the achievement of both project-specific monitoring and statewide evaluation. But as the central agency focused on its main priority, the other aspects tended to be overlooked. And because of the ambivalent and sometimes awkward relations between the project and central agency staffs, the output disappointed both federal authorities and project managers.

Source: World Bank.

National monitoring and evaluation based on socioeconomic indicators of long-term macro changes should be carried out by a central unit in conjunction with national facilities for data collection and processing. Central evaluation of a set of projects can be undertaken with project assistance, if the information which can reasonably be expected from individual projects will allow evaluation analysis, even though it is not ideally suited for this purpose. Such information can be supplemented by special studies contracted to nonproject agencies, as long as their role is clearly stated and agreed to by managers at various levels.

Central evaluation capabilities take time to develop, however. In the interim, therefore, resources for a substantial evaluation capability need to be incorporated into projects. The resources and skills required should not be underestimated, which is why we advocate that this option be used selectively, and only after careful consideration of the need for formal impact analysis that takes into account the size, innovativeness, and risks associated with the project.

Situating Monitoring and Evaluation Systems within a Management Hierarchy

We have made the case that monitoring must be seen as integrated with management, that it is an essential part of good management practice, and that evaluation is linked to monitoring but distinct from it. The need for such integration of monitoring and management is easily stated and is commonly—though not universally—accepted as a principle. In practice, it is not so simple to arrange the appropriate location for the monitoring and evaluation functions within the structures of project management and national authority. Difficult institutional problems may occur with this management-oriented approach, particularly in complex projects involving several different agencies.

Example 3 describes the management system for a set of rural development projects coordinated by a regional authority. A multilayered hierarchy of management included the national agencies, regional authority, the state coordination committee, and such powerful state executing bodies as the extension agency. Which locations were appropriate for monitoring and evaluation in such a case? In fact, they were linked in a single unit, perceived by the executing agencies as being the surveillance arm of the regional authority. The head of each executing agency within a state, however, had his own monitoring system (whether formally designated as such is immaterial), which was intended to meet both his own requirements and his reporting responsibilities to *his* national authorities.

EXAMPLE 3. The Location of Monitoring and Evaluation

The monitoring function, when situated outside the agencies responsible for actual implementation, often serves only to collate and standardize information rather than to guide routine implementation decisions.

A regional authority has the particular mandate to fund projects within states to meet the needs of the rural poor. These projects are executed through a complex administrative hierarchy involving numerous federal, regional, state, and local executing agencies. The regional authority monitors the progress of both its own program and the various agency activities through a technical unit created for each project. But the poverty projects are only a small part of the agencies' wide-ranging activities, which require them to have their own management information systems and reporting mechanisms to fulfill their responsibilities to the state and federal governments.

Because the monitoring of the poverty projects is assigned to the technical unit of the regional authority, however, the executing agencies tend to regard it as merely a clerical task of forwarding information to the technical unit. It is therefore not integrated into the agencies' existing information systems but is a parallel function regarded simply as "reporting."

Moreover, the technical unit is basically seen as an arm of the regional authority and finds it difficult to provide feedback to the executing agencies so that they can adjust their implementation strategies. Nor is the technical unit equipped to collect supplementary data on beneficiary response without the assistance of agency staff. Consequently, the unit tends to become merely to collate information received from agencies and to standardize it into progress reports for the regional authority.

The use of monitoring as a management tool for decisionmaking is therefore largely limited to the internal system maintained within each agency. But this may not reflect the emphasis on the alleviation of poverty, and the information collected passes through a channel independent of the regional authority.

Source: World Bank.

In a regional multistate program, it is both feasible and desirable to provide for monitoring and evaluation of a program or projects and simultaneously to have a series of management information systems in the individual agencies to form basis for these functions. Confusion arises when the unit designed to serve the management of the entire program is perceived as also serving the individual managements of the executing agencies. In another project, which involved eleven agencies, the project monitoring and evaluation unit was originally to be located within *one* of the agencies yet somehow be responsible for these functions in all the agencies.

Resolution of the confusion requires clear specification of management authority. In some cases, the project manager is indeed what the title implies—directly responsible for the execution of the project and its components. In such cases, the monitoring, and to some extent the evaluation, system must serve his or her information needs. But in other cases the project manager simply coordinates the activities of several agencies that deliver particular components of the project with considerable autonomy. In these circumstances, it is important to recognize when designing the project information systems that there is a series of submanagers, each of whom has specific information needs that must be considered first. Established agencies will already have some kind of monitoring and evaluation system, even if it is not recognized as such, and the issue is one of improving and modifying it. In the case of agencies that have been created, or substantially modified for their role in the project, it is necessary to design new systems. Only when these subsystems have been reviewed and their content established can the information system for the coordinating project manager be determined.

Even in a vertical line of command, with a national manager responsible for a project executed by zonal or district officers, it is equally necessary to follow the above model. The information collected must first serve the particular needs of the zonal submanagers before it moves up as an input to the national system.

Project Management View of Evaluation

One of the themes of this book is the necessity to keep ambitions for project evaluation modest. In concluding this overview of monitoring and evaluation from the perspective of project management, we illustrate the limited use of evaluation as a tool for project management.

Evaluation, as defined at the beginning of this chapter, is a broad concept. It covers periodic reviews by the management team as well as more formally designated processes at fixed points in time, such as midterm evaluation, terminal evaluation, and ex post evaluation. If the project has been carefully appraised—that is, there is a strong a priori assumption that certain stimuli and inputs will achieve certain results—the role of management, at least in the early implementation phase, is to create the conditions that will allow this chain of events to occur. The emphasis initially will be on monitoring the input delivery systems and their ability to reach the targeted beneficiaries. Once management is satisfied that these systems are working in accordance with expectations, its attention will shift to the reactions of the beneficiaries and the outputs generated by them. But the emphasis throughout the implementation period will be on regular, timely, pragmatic information supplied to assist in management decisionmaking. This information will often reveal the necessity of examining a project's continued relevance or the overall effectiveness of the intervention strategies adopted. If demand for project services expands as predicted, however, the information may indicate that the target population perceives certain benefits accruing to it and that the project is instrumental in bringing about these benefits. Such internal evaluations are a valid part of the management process. But formal impact evaluation, which measures the change that has come about and the proportion of this change attributable to the project, is another matter. It is time-consuming and requires information that is not a feasible basis for the manager's decisions about implementation. Indeed, it is only seldom feasible for purposes of national or external financing institutions—but it is commonly demanded for them.

Project managers are aware, even without the mathematical proof, that it is difficult to detect an annual production increment of 4–5 percent within the average time span of an agricultural project when there are, say, annual variations of 15–20 percent caused by exogenous forces (common in rain-fed tropical conditions). The managers also know that the evaluation of their performance and that of their project will be made within this time span. Given that the impact of a project can be assessed only at its full development, that is, some years after its completion, and that the manager has to fulfill clearly specified tasks within the limited budget and time frame, the manager and his staff are more concerned with the efficiency of input delivery than about benefits and impacts to be derived in the future.

These issues are considered in greater depth in later chapters; but it is important to note here that the very limited ambitions held by project managers for impact evaluation in agricultural development are not only their pragmatic response to short-term preoccupations but are soundly based in the feasibility of data collection and analysis. It is not that project managers unreasonably fail to provide the data required for formal impact evaluation, but that many evaluators do not understand the inability of information systems to meet their demands, despite the allocation of considerable resources.

Only if priority is given to a monitoring function designed to meet the needs of management can serviceable, realistic, cost-effective information systems be developed. Such systems will not only assist project managers but will provide much data for a realistic and modestly conceived evaluation.

2 | Monitoring and the Management Information System

THIS AND THE NEXT TWO CHAPTERS apply the perspective outlined in chapter 1 to monitoring and its use of a management information system. We first consider how to design and set up a system. The subject is treated in general; precise designs for information systems may differ from project to project depending on each project's objectives, nature, and environment.

System Design

Provision for constructing, maintaining, and using an information system needs to be made when a project is designed. But full specification of the system at this stage may not be consistent with our recommendation that the project management team be closely involved in deciding the contents and range of the system required to meet their needs. In considering this dilemma it is necessary to distinguish between the two most common ways to design an information system—which may be called the "blueprint" and "process" approaches by analogy with the terms for two types of development project.

For the blueprint approach, the project planning and appraisal team or consultants formulate detailed organizational and work plans before project implementation. These plans specify the system's objectives, the required data, the studies to be undertaken, the organizational placement, and the personnel and budgetary needs. Sometimes the plans also include actual survey designs and instruments. The information system is designed according to these plans, and the project staff is expected to adhere to them.

This approach may not give either project managers or monitoring staff enough flexibility to respond to unexpected information needs that may arise during implementation. Data collection may be undertaken within a framework that is overtaken by events. Such problems frequently arise because all contingencies cannot be predicted; the experts prepare the blueprint on the assumption that everything in the project, including risks and difficulties, will proceed as envisaged.

When the blueprint requires a time series of comparable data collected with consistent methods, it is difficult to make changes to accommodate new data needs without putting at risk the original time series. Example 4 describes an extreme case: a longitudinal study maintained despite its increasing irrelevancy to the pressing problems of the project.

EXAMPLE 4. Responding to Project Needs

The monitoring and evaluation unit of an integrated agricultural development project was reluctant to change its focus from an ambitious farm survey to the problems of the project's credit component. As a result, project management lacked the information to correct the problems.

The purpose of the farm survey was to estimate crop production functions in order to determine the causalities of observed changes. The survey was carried out over eight crop seasons and thus required consistency over an extended time. Year after year a set sample of farmers was interviewed. It was assumed that they would borrow one year, increase their yields, repay their loans, and borrow again. Enumerators collected data from the farmers without questioning their status within the credit program. When the project began to encounter difficulties in identifying the number of farmers participating in the credit program, the unit was asked to provide the needed information. As some 80 percent of the farmers who participated in one year dropped out the next, the survey was gathering information on farmers who no longer borrowed under the project's credit program.

Requests from higher-level authorities repeatedly stressed the need for information on the reasons behind the high dropout rate. The unit, however, was committed to carrying out the survey, which by now was running into problems with the quality and processing of data.

Finally, as the project collapsed, an ad hoc attempt was made to interview farmers regarding their perceptions of the project. But even at the time of final evaluation little information was available on the crucial failure of the credit scheme. Nor was any output available from the detailed but now irrelevant survey.

Source: World Bank.

The blueprint approach gives project staff little or no direct input into formulating the plans and programs for monitoring and evaluation. Even when the plans are drawn up by consultants after the management team is formed, this team is too preoccupied with project start-up problems to pay much attention to information requirements. Data collection and analysis plans do not seem a high priority for managers during these early stages of project implementation. A 1985 review of recent World Bank monitoring and evaluation says, "International consultants are still commonly used to . . . design [the] systems . . . but there is a real danger that their presence reinforces the marginal status of M&E activities." The explanation is that managers do not identify with such systems and regard them as distinct from their management concerns.

The process approach, conversely, specifies—but takes an evolutionary view of—fundamental recording requirements for physical and financial monitoring and for evaluation. It gives the planning responsibility to project managers and staff. The project planning team or consultants do not specify plans and work programs. They outline objectives, organizational arrangements, and personnel requirements for the management information system, which includes the essential dimensions of the monitoring and evaluation functions. Specific activities are determined by project managers as their information needs emerge. The process approach makes the information system an effective tool for project managers. It permits them to use their resources to collect and analyze data on the subjects and problems they view as important for project implementation.

The success of the process approach depends largely on the initiative and capability of both the project manager and the monitoring and evaluation staff, for together they shoulder the primary responsibility for innovative planning and efficient implementation. This condition is the main problem with this approach: projects in developing countries face a dearth of qualified and experienced staff. It is difficult to recruit local professionals with the necessary skills and initiative, and it is almost impossible to keep them in a monitoring role. The blueprint approach is thus more practical in such cases.

The blueprint approach is also preferable for physical delivery projects in which implementation problems are essentially technical or managerial and can be mapped in advance. It has been found eminently suitable for such infrastructure development initiatives as the construction of dams, irrigation canals, roads, silos, or housing, in which the phases of the project's growth can be specified in advance and monitored accordingly. It has also been used successfully in extension and forestry projects.

In many instances a monitoring information system can incorporate both approaches. A broad design for the system can be blueprinted at the appraisal stage, and throughout the implementation process the staff can exercise considerable flexibility in responding to new challenges and opportunities.

Examples 5 and 6 illustrate the contrasting approaches that may be used taken at the project planning stage.

EXAMPLE 5. A Blueprint Approach for a Credit Project

The following is a summary from a project preparation document of the design of a monitoring and evaluation system for a credit project. It specifies four distinct components of the system.

The financial monitoring component *provides a set of formats for monthly reporting by bank branches of loan applications, approvals, and disbursements and for semiannual reporting by branches of loan recoveries. A format is also provided for monthly and cumulative aggregate analysis of loan output. The recipients of each report are listed, and the issues to be discussed at management meetings are specified.*

The institutional monitoring component *tracks the performance of bank branches in efficiently delivering loans and in adequately managing the line of credit for each proposed area of lending. A format is provided for quarterly and cumulative reporting of performance indicators. Again, recipients of the reporting system are identified.*

The ongoing evaluation component *routinely records the progress of the significant activities for which the loan was made. A set of daily recording formats is presented for grain mills, oilseed mills, stores, and dairy herds. These records will be maintained by the cooperatives' officials and will be collected by loan officers during their semiannual supervision visits and forwarded to the monitoring and evaluation division. The ongoing evaluation of the oxen sector will be undertaken through a special survey. The main form of analysis of the daily record data will be a reappraisal of the viability of the activity, which will then be compared with the original loan appraisal. The semiannual ongoing evaluation reports for each separate loan will be sent to the cooperatives, the appropriate credit branch, and other authorities. When the analysis indicates problems, the report will be flagged for immediate action.*

The impact evaluation component *consists of a series of end-of-project studies based on the aggregate of information generated by the monitoring and evaluation systems, and a set of special studies concerning particular project components. The end-of-project studies will be concerned with the performance of credit banks in relation to loan management, the viability of project lending activities in each sector, and the impact of lending on dairy production and consumption. The special studies will not be based on large-scale surveys but will use small case study samples to generate assessments of impact. The special studies include the socioeconomic characteristics of grain mill users (to be undertaken by local consultants), the use of surpluses generated by project-financed activities, and the impact of work oxen on agricultural production.*

In the project, recommendations were made to bring the available professional staff to specified strength by certain target dates. Training was recommended and specified in terms of courses and locations for the majority of the new monitoring personnel, and three consultancies were identified with specification of terms of reference during the project.

Source: IFAD.

EXAMPLE 6. A Process Approach for an Agriculture Project

An agriculture project was designed to test possible strategies to improve farming practices. The appraisal report proposed a flexible approach to accommodate information needs as the project developed:

There is no standardized "blueprint" for the development of upland agriculture and conservation practices. Rather, the central operational concept of the project is learning-by-doing, which depends on the capacity to monitor the project's output. The establishment of provincial and district Management Information Systems (MIS) capable of routinely generating data on output performance and providing information to project authorities is, therefore, a central component of the project. Accordingly, an effective management information system will be required prior to expanding the project into additional districts.

In addition to the MIS for daily management, project staff and technical assistance personnel at province and district levels will carry out annual assessments that examine reasons for success or failure of each component activity and will recommend modifications.

The internal annual assessment and planning process undoubtedly will uncover many issues that will require additional data and analysis before action recommendations can be formulated. To address these issues, the project will fund short-term (three months or fewer) special studies through appropriate local institutions or consultants.

Several external evaluations, independent of project authorities, will be carried out during the life of the project. These evaluations will reappraise project concepts, design, allocation of funds, staffing patterns, and component activities in light of the previous year's performance.

Source: U.S. Agency for International Development (USAID).

Information Users and Their Needs

As suggested in chapter 1, the setting up of an information system should be a participatory process involving each level of management. The participants should include officials of the concerned ministries, project managers, executing agency staff, and intended beneficiaries of the project (if institutions and organizations such as farmers' clubs, credit unions, or water users' associations already exist). Their active involvement not only encourages a more representative and responsive design, but also builds communication networks and relationships which can contribute later to the wider diffusion and better utilization of the findings and recommendations of the monitoring process. Example 7 illustrates such a case.

EXAMPLE 7. Encouraging Participant Cooperation in Monitoring an Agriculture Project

The cooperation of participants is a key determinant of success in a development project. In the Philippines, a council monitoring a five-year plan for the agricultural development of an irrigation project became an effective decisionmaking body through the skillful use of information and the varied composition of its membership.

The council, which comprised representatives from various agencies, farmers' associations, provincial governments, and the private sector, met monthly to exchange information on project activities. Despite the council's diverse makeup, a collegial atmosphere developed. Members used an information system specially designed to support the council's collective objectives, in order to comment on the monitoring program and make recommendations. The information provided at the meeting was collated from various information sources and included findings unattainable from the participants' own internal management information systems. Participants therefore found it in their own best interests to attend meetings to gain new information, to present their own reports to the council, and to raise issues for discussion.

Broad lines of communication were developed by the council. Implementing agencies used the meetings to transmit important information to the farm population at large through the farmers' representatives. Representatives of the provincial governments took a keen interest in the sessions in order to keep informed on the details of operations within their administrative districts. In the sessions, the opportunity to pose questions to fellow members created a frank atmosphere that helped cooperation.

Moreover, in determining its objectives the council, had recognized the potential value of giving the farmers an equal footing in the discussions. Farmer representatives had access to higher authorities through the council and over time became vocal in expressing their needs. Nongovernmental participants in this administrative environment were then willing to supply information, which gave the council a consistent source of the beneficiaries' perceptions and reactions.

The council functioned successfully because it acted as a forum for tracking the progress of the project as a whole, rather than serving the requirements of individual agencies. Information provided through the council acted as an incentive to gain active participation. The members in turn provided information and insights that enabled coordinated decisionmaking to improve project performance.

Source: Ronald Ng and Francis Lethem, *Monitoring Systems and Irrigation Management: An Experience from the Philippines* (Washington, D.C.: World Bank, 1983).

In view of limited resources of staff, money, and time, the requirements of all users are unlikely to be fully and effectively met by the information system. The management perspective articulated in chapter 1 demands that first priority be given to the monitoring needs of project staff working at various levels of responsibility in project implementation. They should be treated as the primary information consumers. Next come provincial or national government agencies and departments that are responsible for supervising and coordinating projects and meeting the requirements of intended beneficiaries. Then come the demands of funding agencies, other than those demands that clearly have to be met—even though they are somewhat independent of the monitoring and evaluation functions described here—because they are mandated by legal covenants and financial agreements.

Managers at each level of the hierarchy must furnish periodic reports to their superiors. Besides enabling the senior managers to assess performance, these reports give them a history of the project's implementation and highlight problems that require them to act. The project managers in turn prepare regular reports on the progress of the project as a whole which are submitted to the parent organization, central government, and funding agencies. But in recognition of the necessary tradeoff between timeliness and precision, the information that the manager needs in order to manage may be different in coverage, detail, periodicity, and even degree of accuracy from the kind that he or she reports. The reporting format is often determined by procedures prescribed or agreed upon at the outset of the project. The information required from each project unit by the project manager for his or her day-to-day needs is not necessarily consistent with this format.

The reporting procedures that relate directly to a manager's accountability are inevitably more developed than those for internal monitoring. Both are important, but for successful implementation it is clearly vital that the internal system works well; otherwise formal reporting is more likely to reveal inefficiency and ineffectiveness. The proposed requirements for the internal system need to be identified by the project manager and staff and then reviewed to verify that the preset requirements for reporting to higher authorities can be met. This review may show redundancies and irrelevancies in these latter requirements which, with agreement of all parties, may be eliminated.

It is difficult to determine the information requirements for monitoring, partly because more often than not the users themselves have not decided what they really need. The experience of many projects shows that managers describe topics or issues only in general. One often hears the remark, "We want all relevant information about project implementation." Designers of the information system should therefore try to help managers identify specific items of information. Answers should be sought to such questions as:

- What is the minimum information prerequisite for effective management?
- What are the timing requirements for each information item?
- In what form should the information be conveyed?
- How will the information be used?

Experience also indicates that a conceptual framework assembled by outside experts should not be used to identify information needs. Projects that have not included the needed dialog with users to identify actual needs, or that have merely made a cursory assessment of such needs, have tended to produce expensive systems that are largely irrelevant to the requirements of high-priority users. This is demonstrated by the experience of a rural development project in which the decisionmakers argued that it was up to the experts (in this case academic researchers) to decide what information the managers should have. A review of the monitoring and evaluation system states, "In the absence of clear guidance as to what was and what was not useful, data on over 1,000 village-level variables were collected, far more than could ever be analyzed or used."[1]

High-priority users of information also tend to generate much of the information, which allows a reciprocal relationship to be established between the users and the monitoring staff. For instance, beneficiaries' groups that want a certain type of information from a monitoring system can more readily be persuaded regularly to provide their views on the efficiency and effectiveness of the delivery system. Zonal or agency submanagers routinely record much of the data required both by themselves and, in an agreed summarized form, by the overall project management. In making such arrangements, the following questions are helpful:

- What information can be provided by the user?
- When can it be provided?

1. Maureen Norton and Sharon Benoliel, *Guidelines for Data Collection, Monitoring and Evaluation Plans for Asia and Near East Bureau Projects* (Washington, D.C.: USAID, 1987).

- In what form can it be transmitted?
- What assistance is needed from the monitoring staff to supply this information?

One problem for system designers is that officials or organizations with original access to information are often reluctant to collate and disseminate it. There is a conscious or unconscious tendency to ignore information that warns of poor performance or to exaggerate positive developments. Extension workers, for example, who are in the best position to provide systematic, in-depth data about farmers' responses to the messages delivered, may be the least willing to do so, at least in an objective format, for they fear such information may be used against them. To the extent that project staff supply information to the overall system, the manager has to stress that such information must be verifiable and objectively recorded. Biased data may be more damaging to the system than a gap—which can be filled later by direct data collection.

The Hierarchy of Project Objectives

Identifying the priority of users is the first step in designing an information system. The identification of the users' needs requires a framework for the dialog between the user and system designer. Step two, therefore, is an analysis of the hierarchy of project objectives, in order to determine target populations, critical activities, and tasks to be monitored against agreed targets.

There are both short-term and long-term project objectives. The former define specifically what the project is expected to achieve, for example, improved input services, increased yields, greater production, or more employment opportunities. Long-term objectives are defined in the context of broader sectoral, multisectoral, or national policies. These objectives are to achieve sustained development consistent with national policies through the attainment of the short-term objectives. In the case of agriculture and rural development projects, the long-term objectives are often described in terms of improvement in the living conditions of the rural population and alleviation of poverty. Some projects simply stress production or service delivery goals.

Project objectives are set out in the planning and appraisal documents, as in example 8; if not given explicitly, they can be derived from them. Both explicit and implicit objectives should be taken into consideration. It should be recognized that the objectives, especially the short-term ones, may need to be modified during implementation either because of changes in the external environment or the pace of change (or lack of it) brought about by the implementation process itself.[2] A project with an initial objective of providing short-term credit to 5,000 farm households may have to modify its objective if a rise in interest rates causes the demand for credit to drop. An objective to expand production of one crop at the expense of another may have to be modified because of government price policy changes outside the influence of the project. Or a project service may be so enthusiastically adopted that the objective of reaching half the targeted population may need to be raised.

EXAMPLE 8. Specification of Project Objectives

The following is an example of how project objectives were set out in an appraisal report for a rural development project. The statement is weak in two respects: the intended beneficiaries are not precisely identified, and there is no prioritization of a mixed set of rural operations.

The project would support two important government objectives:

- *Strengthening rural development institutions at national, provincial, and village levels*
- *Improving living conditions and incomes in rural areas through the implementation of selected high-priority rural operations not being undertaken under existing projects and programs and for which no alternative financing is readily available.*

To achieve these objectives, the project would provide financing for institutional development:

- *The strengthening of regional agricultural planning, project preparation, and appraisal capacity*
- *The strengthening of agency management at the central and regional levels*
- *The execution of three priority studies*
- *The establishment of a line of credit for small, high-priority rural activities to be identified under the project to complement ongoing rural development programs.*

In addition, several components were identified:

- *The development of about 1,000 hectares of bottomlands for rice and sorghum cultivation under partial water control in the northern region*
- *The drilling of about 1,000 boreholes for rural water supply*

2. The procedures for approval of such changes and safeguards against alterations designed merely to disguise implementation ineffectiveness need to be well specified. Consideration of these procedures, however, lies outside the scope of this book.

- *A bullock-fattening scheme for about 2,000 farmers*
- *The support of groundnut marketing and shelling*
- *The functional literacy training of village groups*
- *The pilot development of about 20 hectares of bottomlands for vegetable production*
- *The construction and maintenance of about 250 kilometers of access roads in the project area.*

Source: World Bank.

Project objectives can be grouped in four hierarchical categories; various systems differ in their labels for these categories. The previous World Bank handbook[3] described the sequence as inputs, outputs, effects, and impact. In the context of an agricultural investment project, the inputs include such project services as developing infrastructure, improving extension delivery systems, and supplying recommended farm inputs. The outputs include the productivity and other changes in the farming system that result from utilizing these services. The effects are the agroeconomic benefits accruing to the project beneficiaries, and the impact is expressed in terms of changes in the living standards and quality of life of the targeted population and region involved. A similar four-level hierarchy of objectives, known as the logical framework, uses the terms inputs, outputs, purposes, and goals, roughly equivalent to inputs, outputs, effects, and impact.

The precise distinctions between outputs and effects or outputs and purposes vary, not only among writers but also according to whether the project emphasizes investment or technical assistance. We return to these classifications of the hierarchy in chapter 7, but the important issue with regard to monitoring and the content of the management information system is how far it is possible to go in monitoring progress toward the higher-order objectives. Broadly, monitoring should include input delivery, the extent of favorable farmer reaction, and the *initial* indications of output changes and effects on the intended beneficiaries. More precise measurement of effects and measurement of the lasting impact require more formal evaluation studies.

For managers, the focus of the required information system will be on short-term objectives. Measurement of progress toward long-term objectives is more difficult because data on socioeconomic variables must be collected, and it takes considerable time to detect movement in these variables.

3. Dennis J. Casley and Denis A. Lury, *Monitoring and Evaluation of Agriculture and Rural Development Projects* (Baltimore, Md.: Johns Hopkins University Press, 1981).

Once again, the designer of the information system must take into account the limitations of monitoring resources and recognize that the objectives of a project are not all of equal importance. It is necessary to rank as well as classify objectives. In an area development project, for instance, the adoption of a hybrid variety of maize by 60 percent of the small farmers is likely to be perceived as a more important objective than, say, using inoculation services to lower the mortality of young chicks. The information system must ensure that the priority objectives are fully accommodated, if necessary at the expense of those considered secondary.

The Project Intervention Model and Target Specification

In project implementation, progress toward short-term objectives is measured by the achievement of targets for project completion and the adoption of services by the targeted population at various time intervals. Some of these targets will be specified in the project appraisal documents, but others will need to be developed in discussion with managers, particularly in the context of the preparation of annual work plans and budgets. In the appraisal documents some targets, although quantified, may not be easily verified in the short term. For example, yields rising on a steady curve year by year may provide a set of targets, but verification will depend on a lengthy time series. A quantified target that can be verified regularly and without delay as part of monitoring is termed a verifiable target.

It is important that these targets be expressed with reference to the intended beneficiary population and its constituent subgroups, such as smallholders, the rural poor, women farmers, farmers in various locations, and the type of farming system operated. The management information system must include a specification of the size, composition, and situation of the targeted population in order to monitor both the extent to which the project's inputs and services are reaching the intended beneficiaries and how they are responding to these stimuli.

It is also necessary to establish targets for each component of the project. Most agriculture and rural development projects have several components, for example, supply of credit, extension advice, farm inputs, feeder roads, and marketing services. As with the choice of objectives discussed above, priorities may need to be established so that the information system provides for more regular and careful monitoring of progress toward the targets related to the more important components.

Each project is based on an intervention model—whether explicit or not—which explains the relation between a project's inputs and outputs, between outputs and effects, and between effects and impact. The model provides a rationale for the strategy to be used in order to move from the existing conditions toward the desired state.

Some intervention models are well-tested, and their outcomes are predictable under normal circumstances. We know that the introduction of a widely used hybrid variety of maize, along with the recommended units of fertilizer, water, and labor, will increase yields. In such cases, the underlying assumptions are based on experience and can be easily determined. In an innovative project, however, the links between an input and output may be uncertain. No one can be certain that the introduction of a new crop, which requires changes in the accustomed farming system, will be acceptable to the farmers.

The design of the information system should include an examination of the intervention model and the underlying assumptions. This examination helps in the identification of the likely problems in implementation, which in turn assists in focusing the data collection and recording processes on monitoring the emergence of these problems.

The intervention model will have implications for the achievement of certain targets within a given time frame, which is necessary if the underlying assumptions are holding true. The combination of these targets and times assists in specifying the requirements.

Review of Existing Information Systems

Except in innovative projects executed by a new management structure independent of existing agencies (and fortunately these are rare), a systematic, in-depth review of the information systems that antedate the project is the next stage of the design process for two reasons. First, optimal use of available information, both within and outside the project, reduces the need for additional data collection. Second, if the management information system is to function efficiently and effectively, it should improve on existing systems by adapting and supplementing them rather than being a parallel additional system. Such a course lessens the strain of transition; project staff and government officials long accustomed to following a particular system do not feel threatened, and at least their resistance is minimized.

Designers of the information system should pay particular attention to existing provisions for the following:

- Project records and data files related to the budget, financial reporting, and procurement, together with progress reports on physical implementation
- Information flows to and from the executing agencies and the coordinating agency at provincial or regional or central level (budgets, financial and progress reports, reporting requirements)
- Collection and processing of data by specialized agencies—a national statistical office, planning commission, and so forth.

In addition to these formal systems, informal mechanisms for information gathering and dissemination should be identified and reviewed. In all bureaucracies, particularly in developing countries, much relevant and timely information flows through informal channels such as casual meetings, informal discussions, and field visits. It takes time to acquire the insider's status needed to gain access to such networks, so it will most probably not be possible at the design stage to describe them fully. But as the management information system develops, the contribution that informal systems can make by introducing simple documentation should be borne in mind.

The review of the existing systems should address the following questions to determine the modifications and supplements required to meet the needs of the project management information system:

- What types of information are being collected?
- Is the information available for the specific project area?
- Does the information pertain to the population targeted by the project?
- How reliable and valid are the collected data?
- How frequently is the information gathered?
- How much work is involved in data verification, collation, and analysis?
- How is the information communicated at the various existing levels of decisionmaking?
- How is the information currently used?
- How cost-effective is the existing information system?

In some cases, a specific data collection and processing effort is undertaken during the project planning and appraisal stages. These data often are ignored because they have served their initial purpose. But with adaptation, such data may serve as a baseline for the time series to be maintained as the basis for evaluation of the project. At the least they can give essential insights into the project's design and assumptions and thus help ensure that the information system focuses on these assumptions.

Along with existing primary systems maintained by agencies directly connected to the project, certain secondary sources may be usefully tapped. These include published and unpublished studies, statistics, documents, and reports brought out by various departments, agencies, and institutions for their own use. Government health, education, agriculture, and planning departments collect various kinds of statistics, some of which may be relevant for project monitoring and evaluation. In addition, studies undertaken by universities and research institutions may provide valuable insights on various topics relevant to the project. When accessible in their original form, these secondary data occasionally can be reorganized and reanalyzed to focus on the issues of interest to the project.

Supplementary Data Collection and Recording

Once the review of existing systems has been undertaken, the necessary supplements to the information system can be determined. *Guiding Principles* (see preface) lists possible sources of supplementary information.

- The supply, delivery, and accounting records of the project; these are a major source of information if properly collated, summarized, and integrated with other data
- Data collection techniques that can be incorporated into the normal operations of project staff; examples include harvesting of farm trial and demonstration plots, measuring the flow of water to fields or sections, and weighing and measuring children in health clinics
- In-depth case studies of small numbers from the project population in order to understand the reactions of the intended beneficiaries; these investigations are carried out through detailed, open-ended questions and probes rather than structured questionnaires
- Probability sample surveys of a moderate number of farms, households, or individuals; these normally use a set questionnaire with closed, alternative-choice questions and often include objective counts and measurements
- Interviews with principal respondents for information on community characteristics, such as the state of roads, markets, education and health services, and common agriculture or rural infrastructure constraints
- Participant observation studies, for an analysis of the functioning and role of institutions and groupings of the project beneficiaries.

The circumstances in which each of these data sources and collection methods can be utilized are described in the later chapters of this book; the techniques themselves are the primary subject of the companion volume. One simple point needs to be stressed here: data collection for monitoring and evaluation should be pragmatic. The standards of data accuracy and reliability should not be as demanding for a management information system as for experimental studies and academic research. Other considerations, such as timeliness, relevance, and cost-effectiveness, are more important.

The choice of method for collecting the required data will depend on the indicators chosen for monitoring progress toward the specified targets.[4] Monitoring the proportions of beneficiaries responding to project stimuli or services requires probability sampling; the development of an output time series may require different methods of data collection depending on whether estimates of output are based on respondent interviews or objective measurements; problem diagnosis may be successfully achieved by carrying out case studies; and monitoring attitudes and perceptions of beneficiaries may use the more in-depth interviewing implied by participant observation or informant studies.

Decisions on the required standards of accuracy, precision, and reliability, which are expressed in statistical terms as confidence intervals and levels of significance, have great consequences for the size and scale of data collection efforts. In experimental work, it is common to use tests of significance requiring 90–95 percent levels of confidence that the null hypothesis has been disproved (for example, that there is no difference between the experimental and control groups). For routine management, the conclusions drawn by monitoring the information within the system can be based, in most cases, on lower levels of confidence. Managers do not, or should not, demand that indicators of project progress should be based on odds of 20 to 1 in favor of any reported change being significant. They might well settle for odds such as 4 to 1, implying an 80 percent confidence level. This is especially the case in three situations: first, when there are multiple sources of information to corroborate the findings; second, when there is a high probability of the sequential deepening of information; and third, when project designs can be modified at a later stage as a result of cumulative feedback.

The initial design should not attempt to specify all the indicators and studies to be incorporated into the information system, unless there is a deliberate decision to adopt a detailed blueprint approach, as discussed earlier. But the designers should indicate the range of indicators to be covered, the relative emphasis to be given to maintenance of routine time series indicators as compared with detailed ad hoc studies, and the appropriate level of detail of data recording and scale of supplementary data collection.

Structure and Resources

Even if the process approach is adopted and there is thus considerable latitude for development of the system during project implementation, it

4. Of course, there are other considerations; for example, a bigger or risky project may require more elaborate, precise data.

is necessary at the project design stage to integrate the information system into the management structure and to allocate staff and budget.

Some components of the information system, particularly physical and financial data, will be recorded and maintained within the project management structure, which is discussed further in the next chapter. In the simplest projects there may be no need for a unit to draw the information together and provide the monitoring services to the various user levels. But in most projects such a unit is provided for, which also encompasses at least part of the evaluation function (hence the ubiquitous title M&E unit).

The required staffing for this purpose needs to be carefully specified. If the emphasis is on routine monitoring of physical and financial performance, a team of economists is not likely to provide the appropriate skills. Conversely, the efficient collection and interpretation of farm data require staff with experience and skills in farming systems and agricultural economics.

Special attention should be given to the size of the technical staff. Although the size depends on the nature of a project, its information needs, and the resources available, a small, compact team is preferable to a large one, whose management itself becomes a problem. If coordinated properly, a multidisciplinary team is a major asset because it can articulate different perspectives and thus give a fuller, more balanced picture of the project. But the operation of the information system should not become a forum for fighting disciplinary battles. To avoid this, an important consideration in the recruitment of technical staff and the specification of their terms of reference is emphasis on a practical orientation, with the team seen as a service unit organized to contribute to efficient project management and implementation.

It is also desirable to avoid establishing a large force of permanent supervisors and enumerators for collecting data in a project-specific context, although there will be exceptions when such a force is justified. There are several reasons for this. First, full-time enumerators and supervisors are costly. Even when the salaries are low, the opportunity cost of the resources spent on enumerators and their logistical support should not be ignored. Second, in most instances, there will not be adequate continuous work for the enumerators. The enumerators are busy only when the data are being collected, although this problem is alleviated if they can also edit and process the data. Third, the management of a large field force involves additional administrative responsibilities that put a strain on a small professional team and diverts it from the main task of data analysis, interpretation, and dissemination. In some cases, temporary enumerators and supervisors can be employed for specific studies and surveys, although this adds to the training requirements.

A frequent omission at the design stage is consideration of data storage, processing, and retrieval requirements. Surveys are called for with reference to sizes of samples and so forth, but assessment of the resources required to digest the incoming data and turn them into management information is often neglected. The use of microcomputers is becoming more feasible and cost-effective; they have proved their usefulness in many projects. Nevertheless, the switch to such technology from manual or simple calculator systems can bring problems in its wake. We recommend that in such a changeover the old system be maintained in parallel until the initial problems of the computer system are overcome.

Three aspects of staffing are of critical importance. First, agreement must be reached in detail on the location of the staff responsible for maintaining the management information system and using it to monitor the project. Second, the staff's reporting responsibilities to project managers must be clearly delineated. Third, the staff's role in disseminating information to the project team as well as providing feedback to beneficiary groups must be articulated. In addition, the formats of reports and their timing should be specified. The superficial response to this requirement is merely to specify the production of quarterly or annual reports, which may go largely unread by busy managers. The essence of an effective management information system is the ability to supply succinct regular outputs of progress in simple formats, to detect the emergence of unexpected developments, and to draw these developments to the attention of those who can respond.

The best strategy for attaining these goals is to initiate at an early stage a number of workshops involving project managers, monitoring and evaluation staff, and other potential information users. Such workshops can examine the information needs of the different users, identify specific information items, formulate communication strategies, and negotiate respective responsibilities. The details of technical issues—such as the formulation of indicators, techniques of statistical analysis, and specific survey methodologies—should not be discussed in such workshops. These can be dealt with by the technical staff in the light of the agreed-upon communication strategies.

Once the management information system starts functioning, such workshops should be held annually to review progress and suggest necessary changes in the light of experience or a changing environment. In some management structures, the review of the information emanating from the system, which will lead to the preparation or revision of work schedules, may be formalized within a committee. Such a committee can also review the flow of the information within the project team to ensure that the appropriate facts are available to the relevant users at the correct time.

Cost of the Information System

It is unrealistic to give specific cost figures for a management information system because staff and equipment requirements will vary according to the objectives and extent of the project as well as the project management structure. Costs for providing a given resource vary widely from country to country. Example 9 provides a summary distribution of resources provided for monitoring and evaluation in recent World Bank–funded projects, although this distribution needs to be interpreted cautiously because government inputs of existing staff and equipment often are not included. Furthermore, some of the more richly endowed cases set very high objectives for evaluation, which nevertheless failed; we would not have advocated such ambitious attempts and so would have preferred the allocation of fewer resources to meet more realistic purposes.

EXAMPLE 9. Costs for Monitoring and Evaluation in Selected Agriculture Projects

Cost component (thousands of dollars)	Percentage of projects
Less than 200	19
200–500	35
501–1,000	24
1,001–2,500	15
2,501 and above	7
Total	100

The agriculture projects in the sample are large: they often have total project costs of $100 million or more. The funds for monitoring and evaluation may not seem excessive in this context, although more than 20 percent of the projects established monitoring and evaluation units with costs of more than $1 million (usually to cover a project of five to six years' duration).

Source: World Bank.

The following describes, as an example only, the type of monitoring unit we envisage in an average development project:

- One graduate monitoring officer (MO) to oversee the management information system and to disseminate its output
- Two technical staff workers to assist the MO, one for computing and analysis, the other to oversee beneficiary contact surveys and diagnostic studies (see chapters 3 and 4)
- Sufficient junior staff (six to eight persons) to form two or three mobile teams to undertake the necessary data collection and basic tabulation
- Support staff, such as one clerk and one or two drivers

- Adequate transport for the field teams; this may require a minimum of one vehicle and a few motorbikes; too frequently a monitoring and evaluation unit is overendowed with staff, none of whom has the means to move about
- Data processing and tabulation equipment, which frequently includes one microcomputer—if so, there should be adequate provision for the purchase of the required software, plus any necessary consultancy funds for setting up the processing system and training the unit staff.

If a formal evaluation is included (in accordance with a review of the need as discussed in chapter 1), the resources and therefore costs are likely to escalate by a factor of three or four. Even if such an impact study is contracted to a national institution, the cost of the contract is likely to be greater than the cost of monitoring the project. Not even outline estimates can be given for such studies, which will range from a few in-depth case studies to longitudinal surveys over many years covering several hundred respondents with multiple visits to each respondent in a single year. We need scarcely repeat that we believe the latter should not be the norm.

3 | Monitoring of Physical and Financial Progress

THE COORDINATED MONITORING of physical and financial information is essential for the efficient implementation and operation of any development project. While most project managers well understand the basic principles of physical and financial monitoring, it is often seen to be so routine that, as stated in chapter 1, it is omitted from discussions of monitoring and evaluation. This part of the management information system and its use must, however, be recognized as the basis for the development of the complete monitoring function.

Fundamentals of Physical and Financial Monitoring

Although records are kept by all management entities, the information generated may not always be used for internal monitoring. Most record-keeping systems are designed to help managers report to higher authorities or comply with other external requirements.

The issue of reporting for external use has been addressed earlier in this volume; this chapter concentrates on the internal use of information by managers. Record-keeping systems fundamentally are concerned with work performed and expenditure incurred. These systems, which may be quite elaborate, include an accounts section to deal with budgetary planning and control and a parallel reporting system to track the progress of physical work and generate a regular series of internal and external reports.

We draw a sharp distinction between information required from project managers and information needed by project managers. The hierarchical flow of information on project progress is reflected in the management structure itself; what is needed by one level has to be provided by the immediately lower level. The chain extends up from the point of action through the management system to the highest level of responsibility. At each level, the information should be reviewed, its deviations from expectations noted, and necessary action taken before it is transmitted further upward in a more aggregated form. Too often the information flows through the management system without these vital steps being performed. Even the necessary aggregation is often neglected. The result of this passive upward transmission of data is that higher-level managers receive information with important facts buried in excessive detail. When the information is finally reviewed by senior managers, it may be discovered that actions should have been taken earlier at lower levels.

Efficient and effective physical and financial performance depends upon deploying resources and executing tasks to achieve targets and objectives in a given time. The use of project services depends on their availability, which in turn depends on the efficient generation of these services. Therefore, a primary aspect of monitoring a project is to review the physical and financial resources which are to be the source of benefits and the means of achieving objectives. This review requires the generation of physical and financial information, at varying frequencies, about the availability and deployment of both staff and equipment (including its serviceability); about progress in constructing infrastructure (for example, roads, buildings, and irrigation works); about the development of project services (for example, nurseries, seed multiplication, and extension advice delivery systems); and about the availability and distribution of inputs (for example, fertilizers, seeds, and credit activities). The review must take into account the requirements for an appropriate balance and timing of supply and demand; cash flows (inflows and outflows) for specific revenue-generating components; and budget provisions and expenditures by activity and component and for the project as a whole.

As stated earlier, looked at in isolation, standard record keeping within the system that generates only physical and financial reporting has limited operational meaning; operational relevance requires that the data be compared with benchmarks and targets. Physical and financial performance is related to, indeed is defined by, the degree to which targets and objectives are achieved at specific times in the life of a project. Some of these targets and objectives will be specified in the original project document; others will be set out in the annual work plans and schedules drawn up by project staff during the implementation of a project, as introduced in chapter 2.

To appreciate the relation between information and project targets, and the timing implications, we again consider the principles of project management. A manager's basic responsibilities, which were described in chapter 1, are planning, organizing, motivating, and controlling. Monitoring deals mostly with the first and last of these. Controlling includes gathering information on actual progress and performance, assessing deviations from targets, analyzing possible causes, and taking remedial action. Managers of complex projects cannot be directly involved in all these functions; tasks are delegated so that the managers can plan and decide on remedial actions. The process of identifying both positive and negative deviations is crucial for monitoring. Moreover, linkages to planning, in which standards are applied and targets set, and to other elements of controlling are critically important. Monitoring can be effective only insofar as the plans themselves are realistic; it is essential for those responsible for monitoring to be intimately involved in planning.

Controlling a project also involves monitoring its legal requirements and such procedures as those for tendering and procuring equipment materials and services. The project manager as controller is also concerned with achieving targets efficiently. Work records and time sheets will reveal underutilized resources, overstaffing, and surplus supplies. The cost-effectiveness of project activities is of prime importance; it is thus necessary to monitor their unit costs through formal cost accounting.

Operation of Physical and Financial Monitoring Systems

A project manager requires regular information on each project activity to ensure that the project is being implemented effectively and to detect and correct deviations from the project plan. Progress reporting and financial accounting may not always meet this need because they focus more on external reporting than internal monitoring (see discussion earlier in chapter 2). Traditional information systems are often geared to satisfying the administrative requirement that funds and resources be adequately accounted for and work assignments accomplished. If these systems function reasonably well, relatively little effort is required to slightly modify them so that line managers can do the necessary monitoring. Some of the adjustments are obvious, but others can be detected only by careful examination.

Perhaps the most common deficiency of management information systems is that deviations from planned physical and financial targets may not be traceable to specific line managers or cost centers and therefore the origin of a problem cannot be readily identified. Valuable time for action can be lost if a special investigation is needed to pinpoint the source of a problem. For example, a shortage in the project stores of fertilizer for distribution before the planting season begins can be detected from the stock control reports of any functional management information system. But it may not be known whether the problem was caused by inadequate transport, by the late placement of orders or even by an underestimation of demand. In a good monitoring system, such attribution should be possible. Or a project manager may find from summary reports that expenditure on fuel for the project has exceeded the budgeted level by a significant margin. In the absence of information on which cost center is responsible for the overrun, his only option is to issue general instructions to all operational units to economize on fuel consumption. The consequence may be a reduction of critical field activities, even by units that were operating efficiently. Furthermore, belated investigations and general strictures are not only inefficient, but also harmful to staff morale.

Organizing a project on the basis of cost centers is fundamental for cost accounting. This comparatively modern concept is distinct from traditional financial accounting in that it is an internal management tool whereas financial accounting basically meets the needs of external reporting. Both types of accounting depend on the same project accounts but differ in how the information is used. Cost accounting describes the relationships between costs incurred on inputs of resources and materials for specific activities and the planned outputs and services from those activities. It was developed in manufacturing and merchandising to facilitate product costing and pricing and soon evolved into a powerful tool for monitoring financial progress. Cost accounting promotes the coordination of operations, contributes to performance monitoring, and facilitates management decisionmaking.

Cost accounting deals only with the variable costs of a task plus that portion of the fixed costs attributable to specific activities. Thus it does not replace financial accounting. Conventional accounting methods tend to reflect auditable full costs, so that in many cases fixed costs obscure controllable costs. A supplementary cost accounting system focuses on controllable costs and uses advance estimates, which enable monitoring to detect impending problems early.

To take full advantage of the potential of such a management information system, the cost centers should directly correspond to the centers responsible for implementation. Such a system may not always coincide with the existing lines of command. If the differences cannot be reconciled, the potential contributions of the management information system are seriously diminished. In extreme cases, some reorganization of the management structure may be necessary.

Although a system of responsibility centers needs to be reviewed in each project, these centers generally perform the following functions:

- Preparing of a work program for certain project implementation activities for a period defined by the project manager
- Preparing of a budget to support the work program which highlights controllable costs
- Exercising of full responsibility for execution of the specified activities
- Reporting to higher-level managers on physical and financial progress for these activities.

On the basis of these functions, a project manager must decide on the system of responsibility centers that best serves his and the project's needs.

Data in the System

Given a management information system adapted to meet the monitoring needs outlined above, the data to be included in the system need to be determined. General criteria include the following.

- Physical and financial data should consist mainly of direct physical and financial quantities for each activity. Proxy indicators have little place in this aspect of monitoring, although percentages may be useful, particularly for allocated funds actually spent compared with budgeted amounts.
- Priority should be given to data on the performance of tasks for which precise targets can be set. Targets for physical performance will be specified in the work program. Financial targeting requires a focus on controllable costs.
- Data on physical performance need to be related to budgeted costs to ensure that the objectives are reached at acceptable actual costs.
- Emphasis should be placed on data relating either to activities that are critical to the achievement of further tasks (see below) or to activities which experience has shown are most prone to delays or cost overruns caused either by internal problems or exogenous forces such as price changes.

These criteria apply both to the monitoring of a project by its manager and to the reporting of progress to higher levels. Although a project manager may need the full details to pinpoint problems, there will certainly be more aggregation in presentation to higher authorities. As one ascends the hierarchy of management the data should become aggregated so that the project may be reviewed as an entity, and the use of percentage indicators of performance against targets becomes more prominent.

For internal project monitoring, the information system will also need to emphasize two additional criteria:

- The data for monitoring progress must be sensitive to change over short periods.
- The information should highlight those aspects that can be influenced by action within managers' operational discretion.

The monitoring system should not focus on what may be interesting but on what is absolutely necessary for the manager to know. The complexity of a project, not its scale, determines the elaborateness of the system. A multicomponent area development project obviously requires more progress indicators than a project within a single technical subsector.

An area development project in China, for example, uses a system of more than a hundred indicators for physical progress reporting, but the project has fifteen major components. Progress of most components is tracked by fewer than ten indicators—in some cases even as few as two or three.

When project implementation is carried out by several agencies, each with a different and independent information system, the project management unit may have to transfer the information into a standardized format or require each agency to provide the information in a format specially designed for the project.

When a project manager has the authority to design the system and ensure compliance with it, it will reflect his management style. This style may involve tight control of activities; such is often the case with irrigation schemes. Other managers place considerable emphasis on rapid communications. The monitoring of water delivery is often conducted with field radio telephones, but real-time communication is not restricted to irrigation operations. Example 10 gives two quotations. The first stresses the tight operational control exercised by a manager of an irrigation project, which reflects his requirement for precise schedules and active monitoring in accordance with them; the second is an extreme case of the management requirement for rapid and constant communication over a large area that is ill-served by normal communication facilities. We do not argue that such tight control and constant communications are a requirement in all cases, but the quotations do dramatize the difference between record keeping and active monitoring.

EXAMPLE 10. Examples of Active Physical Monitoring

"This successful performance [of the project] stems largely from the highly efficient and effective system of management which maintains a tight control of project operations. This greatly facilitates monitoring of the project. All project staff have clearly defined roles and precisely specified tasks and they operate within a managerial system which continuously evaluates its own performance. The . . . management system comprises six sub-systems relating to tractor operations, water control, crop production, and handling, maintaining and repair of structures, accounting and the management of tenants . . . Management efficiency is greatly enhanced by the generation of appropriate information and rapid response to it. All the sub-systems are closely monitored by the project staff and the data thus generated allow project operation [and] performance . . . to be measured . . . and remedial responses to be ef-

*fected when necessary . . . A well-designed information transmittal system
ensures that the right information is provided at the right frequency, in the
right place, and at the right time. The monitoring system [provides] information to enable decisions to be taken away from the center. At the same time,
information flows into the center which keeps the manager informed . . . and
enables him to take direct action when this becomes necessary."*

Source: Eric Clayton, *Agriculture, Poverty, and Freedom in Developing Countries*
(New York: Macmillan, 1983).

*"Every morning each development center had to radio in [a] report. Failure
to call resulted in an immediate visit that day to find out why they had not
called. This had the effect of keeping the staff up to the mark without a physical visit and reduced the cost of administration . . . My vehicle was fitted with
a radio . . . Thus I was never out of touch and could physically control . . .
progress of much of the field work."*

Source: FAO.

Other projects may be more concerned with whether physical objectives are being achieved at acceptable financial costs. In one project
reported by the FAO, financial monitoring involves:

- Recording transactions to allocate accurately all revenue and costs
  within the cost centers
- Budgeting and forecasting by divisional managers according to the
  master budget
- Reporting financial progress to enable managers and the government to compare performance with the budget, examine deviations,
  and take remedial action.

The basic requirement in the system for monitoring financial progress
is that it establish or improve accounting records. In a smallholder coffee
project, for example, the accounting system included cash books for each
beneficiary with entries on receipts and payments to determine the annual payment due to growers. The cash book system for monitoring the
financial progress of beneficiaries is used in many projects, as is reflected
in several FAO-commissioned case studies. If a cash book system cannot
be applied, field staff have to obtain the data directly. Standardized formats are used to transmit the information to managers. A typical format
is shown in example 11. Within the project administration itself, a beneficiary transaction ledger is kept on loans advanced, interest paid, inputs
supplied, and payments made. In view of the large number of records
and the frequent transactions, the systems are usually computerized.
Similar forms of tracking financial progress are found in most farm credit
projects. Credit supply institutions also maintain a general ledger to keep

track of income and expenditure, assets, and liabilities to generate the financial reports and financial ratios (indicators) to assess the soundness of the institution that operates the credit program.

EXAMPLE 11. *A Monthly Credit Record Form*

Province: Cankiri
Distributed credits _____ Month_____ Year_____
County_____

	Corum Cankiri rural development		Production development project		Fallow land decrease project	
	Thousands of TL	Number of farmers	Thousands of TL	Number of farmers	Thousands of TL	Number of farmers
Short-term credit						
Seeds						
Chemicals						
Fertilizers						
Fodder						
Honeycomb						
Cash						
Medium-term credit						
Tractor						
Trailer						
Plow						
Hoe						
Disc harrows						
Drill						
Fertilizer distributor						
Mower						
Thresher						
Tractor sprayer						
Engine-driven sprayer						
Knapsack sprayer						
Irrigation motor and equipment						
Water tank						

	Corum Cankiri rural development		Production development project		Fallow land decrease project	
	Thousands of TL	*Number of farmers*	*Thousands of TL*	*Number of farmers*	*Thousands of TL*	*Number of farmers*
Medium-term credit						
Barn (new)						
Barn (restructured)						
Calf						
Poultry house						
Hives						
Cattle						
Sheep, goats						
Cows						
Chicks						
Total credit						

Source: FAO.

Up this point, monitoring has been outlined in terms of information from common systems of record keeping and reporting. But an efficient monitoring system needs to address implementation scheduling and costing in an integrated and dynamic manner. The remainder of this chapter discusses an analytical method to facilitate this which we believe will become more popular with managers as the use of microcomputers becomes widespread.

Scheduling and Costing Analysis

The implementation of a project component or principal activity usually involves a number of tasks. Some can be executed simultaneously to save time and to avoid idle resources. But some cannot start until another is completed. The sequential relationships among tasks to be performed by different responsibility centers can thus become very complex; errors in interpreting the interdependence of the tasks and inefficiencies in scheduling can be very costly if they extend completion time and disrupt coordination between different responsibility centers.

Project managers, of course, have always tried to capture the advantages of executing tasks simultaneously. They have traditionally relied on experience as well as clear perception of the relationships among the constituent tasks. The analytical tools for facilitating this process are, however, only of recent origin, although they have been steadily gaining recognition. One of the best known of these is called the critical path

method (CPM). Another well-known acronym is PERT (program evaluation and review technique). PERT is essentially a type of critical path
analysis that utilizes probability functions to estimate the time required
for individual tasks.

The fundamental principle of critical path analysis is to utilize the parallel execution of tasks so as to arrive at the shortest possible implementation period. If the relationships among the tasks are correctly identified, a number of tasks will be seen to need to be undertaken
consecutively; these constitute a path that is followed to reach completion. There could be several of these paths; the longest is known as the
critical path, which determines the duration of the activity. All the tasks
along this path are critical to completing the activity on time; any slip-
page in doing any of them would cause a time overrun of the whole
activity. The planned completion date of each task, particularly those on
the critical path has to be carefully monitored. As those paths which are
not critical are by definition shorter in duration, some of the tasks associated with them would have slack or floating periods. The proper
utilization of the floating time in the network has significant implications
for managers.

In order to use critical path analysis for project planning and monitoring, it is necessary to take certain preliminary steps. These include:

• Listing the constituent tasks of a project activity by responsibility
  center and cost center
• Assessing the time required to complete each task
• Analyzing the logical relationships among, and hence the sequencing of, the tasks
• Estimating the controllable costs and resources required for completing each task.

Simple graphic and numerical techniques are available to aid in identifying the critical and other paths. The methods involved are described in
standard textbooks, for network analysis has become well known and
has many applications in construction and contracting work. Applications to project implementation in developing countries are still relatively
limited, however, largely because the manual construction and analysis
of a task network for even simple projects is taxing and time consuming.
For the same reasons, even if an initial analysis is made, the schedule is
usually not replanned after an early delay, which renders the exercise
null and void. The laborious nature of the work means that the very advantage of critical path analysis, namely, to assist in identifying delays in
order to trigger rescheduling, becomes its main drawback. But the increasing use of microcomputers in project offices and the arrival in the
mid-1980s of user-friendly and powerful software designed for project

management means that the resource constraint to the application of network analysis has largely been removed.

Although there are various techniques for network analysis, the most useful for presenting the sequence of tasks in relation to the implementation calendar is a Gantt chart. In its simplest form, such a chart lists tasks in separate rows and uses horizontal lines to show each task's commencement date, duration, and completion date. The use of a single chart is quite common, but microcomputers and available software can now be used with the chart to arrive at an optimal sequence of tasks and to display the result in different formats. The Gantt chart is used in this way in example 12.

EXAMPLE 12. Use of a Gantt Chart

To distribute fertilizer for a particular crop, the tasks correspond to responsibility centers in the project management structure and their duration and controllable costs are assumed to be as shown in table 1.

Assume that the activity commences in January and has a completion deadline at the beginning of April. The total consecutive duration of the tasks is 124 days, but some obvious overlaps are detectable. The Gantt chart that results from a preliminary analysis is shown in figure 1. The striking feature of this schedule is that seven of the nine tasks are on the critical path; by definition any delay in any of these tasks will result in an extension of the total completion time. The tighter the implementation schedule, the more management attention is required to monitor each task. Moreover, simultaneously undertaking the tasks of ordering fertilizer, repairing storage, and servicing vehicles still fails to get the fertilizer to farmers by the beginning of April.

Table 1. List of Tasks, Durations, and Costs for the Extension Activity

Task	Duration (working days)	Variable costs (thousands of dollars)
1. Deliver fertilizer application message	28	24
2. Assess total quantity required	5	1
3. Order seasonal quantity	2	—
4. Repair storage facilities	14	50
5. Service transport vehicles	14	15
6. Transfer fertilizers to site	15	12
7. Assist farmers to obtain credit	20	5
8. Announce distribution dates	6	2
9. Distribute fertilizer	20	10
Total		119

Figure 1. Fertilizer Distribution Work Schedule

Task	Month																	
	January				February				March					April				May	
Week beginning	6	13	20	27	3	10	17	24	3	10	17	24	31	7	14	21	28	5	12
1. Deliver fertilizer application message.																			
2. Assess total quantity required.																			
3. Order seasonal quantity.																			
4. Repair storage facilities.																			
5. Service transport vehicles.																			
6. Transfer fertilizers to site.																			
7. Assist farmers to obtain credit.																			
8. Announce distribution dates.																			
9. Distribute fertilizer.																			

Key: ──── critical task ── noncritical task ▬ ▬ ▬ available slack time

46

The number of critical tasks can be reduced if vehicle servicing and storage repair are independent of the quantity of fertilizer required, but this revision to the logical sequencing of tasks does not advance the overall completion time (as printing a new version of the chart would reveal). But now it may be decided that the announcement of distribution dates should be announced after the arrival of the fertilizers at the project site rather than the ordering of the fertilizer, since a delay in shipment could force the distribution date to be revised. Also, time could be saved by estimating the approximate quantities required and by initiating work on purchase orders before the end of the first task (the delivery of the extension message); a few days could be left to finalize the estimate later. The results of this planning iteration are presented in figure 2. The completion date for the whole activity is now near the deadline. The critical tasks are the delivery of the extension message, the transfer of fertilizers to the project site, the announcement of the distribution dates, and the actual distribution of fertilizers to the farmers. Further savings in the total duration of the activity must therefore be found among these tasks by reassessing the constraints. Shortening the critical path in this manner is known as crashing. If other possibilities are impractical, the method of distributing fertilizer to the farmers must be modified, for example, by shipping two batches to different parts of the project area. Consequently, the related preceding tasks of announcing dates and shipping fertilizer must be subdivided. There are now twelve identifiable tasks in the final implementation schedule instead of the original nine, as shown in figure 3. The completion date of the activity now meets the planting period. The iterative planning exercise has saved a whole month. Yet only six critical tasks require close monitoring.

If detailed budgets for the controllable expenditure for each task have been prepared, the project manager can now carefully consider the float (slack time) available for some of the tasks and reach a decision on the optimal time for their execution.

We have stressed that style of management has important implications for monitoring. Some managers like to be informed of the commencement of a task within the overall activity, as well as of its progress and completion. Others prefer to delegate responsibility and require only reports on completions. Most managers wish to be informed of both commencement and completion with interim updates only for long-term activities. For critical-path monitoring to be effective, those persons concerned with implementation must understand both the overall logical sequence of tasks and the role of monitoring in ensuring adherence to deadlines. Used in this way, network analysis fosters teamwork, promotes coordination, and encourages commitment. Clearly all persons concerned must be aware of the need to provide an early warning if a task under their control is running late—particularly if it is on the critical path. One of the problems of implementing agriculture projects is the in-

Figure 2. First Improvement of Fertilizer Distribution Work Schedule

Task	Month																
	Week beginning	January				February					March					April	
		6	13	20	27	3	10	17	24	3	10	17	24	31	7	14	21	28
1. Deliver fertilizer application message.																		
2. Assess total quantity required.																		
3. Order seasonal quantity.																		
4. Repair storage facilities.																		
5. Service transport vehicles.																		
6. Transfer fertilizers to site.																		
7. Assist farmers to obtain credit.																		
8. Announce distribution dates.																		
9. Distribute fertilizer.																		

Key: ──── critical task ——— noncritical task ▄▄▄ available slack time

48

Figure 3. Second Improvement of Fertilizer Distribution Work Schedule

Month		January					February					March					April		
Task	Week beginning	6	13	20	27	3	10	17	24	3	10	17	24	31	7	14	21	28
1. Deliver fertilizer application message.																		
2. Assess total quantity required.																		
3. Order seasonal quantity.																		
4. Repair storage facilities.																		
5. Service transport vehicles.																		
6. Transfer fertilizers to site 1.																		
7. Announce distribution dates 1.																		
8. Assist farmers to obtain credit.																		
9. Distribute fertilizers 1.																		
10. Transfer fertilizers to site 2.																		
11. Announce distribution dates 2.																		
12. Distribute fertilizers 2.																		

Key: —— critical task —— noncritical task - - - available slack time flexible schedules that result from the need to provide inputs in accordance with the agricultural seasons. A time overrun of one month in delivery may preclude the adoption of a service for a whole season. Late delivery of fertilizer is an expensive exercise in futility.

If intensive monitoring is desired, a Gantt chart should show tasks with milestones for scheduled commencement dates. A milestone in this context is the critical date on the schedule. But monitoring these milestones requires a rapid flow of information. Although intensive monitoring is required for critical tasks, it may deny the responsibility centers the flexibility to deal with slack time. For managers who delegate responsibility and monitor only the anticipated and actual time of completion, the schedule can be presented according to the temporal order of completion. In the case of a complex activity involving many tasks, it may be decided to monitor only critical tasks. There can be many such permutations. With the software packages now available, it is possible to produce convenient and alternative schedules to suit managers' needs.

Example 12 emphasized the time element of completing the activity. Consider now the variable and controllable costs associated with each task (see table in example 12). The anticipated weekly or monthly expenditure can be calculated as a basis for combined physical and financial monitoring of progress. These costs do not include the cost of the fertilizer or the administrative overhead and staff salaries which are normally beyond the control of the responsibility centers. This illustrates the difference discussed earlier between financial reporting and financial monitoring.

If the project manager chooses to commence all tasks at the earliest possible time, then two-thirds of the variable costs would be incurred in the first month. If the manager prefers to allow the tasks to begin by the latest dates, the expenditure for the first month would drop to below a third of the total and would peak in the second month. If he utilizes the floats available for some of the tasks, then the monthly distribution of expenditure would be more even. In the process, the announcement of the distribution date for the first batch of fertilizer, would become a critical task, while the floats associated with some other tasks would be somewhat reduced. The estimated monthly variable cost totals under these three scenarios are shown in table 2.

Monitoring targeted to the performance of the tasks can now be planned. At the end of February, for example, the project manager needs to know through monitoring that the extension message delivery process is completed; the quantity required has been assessed and ordered; the vehicles have been serviced and the storage facilities repaired; shipment of the first batch of fertilizer has started; the staff has arranged for credit for two-thirds of the intended coverage. Although the activity would not be completed for another five weeks, failure to complete any one of these

Table 2. Alternative Monthly Budget Requirements

Month	Earliest start		Latest finish		Optimal	
	Thousands of dollars	*Percent*	*Thousands of dollars*	*Percent*	*Thousands of dollars*	*Percent*
January	80	67	16	13	37	31
February	19	16	77	65	60	50
March	20	17	26	22	22	19
Total	119	100	119	100	119	100

tasks by the end of February would certainly lead to time or cost over-runs. A time overrun could be serious, for the critical path in the implementation plan has already been crashed so as not to miss the planting season. In the event, succeeding tasks would have to be replanned immediately, either by reducing their duration through over-time work or by further crashing the remaining parts of the critical path. At the end of February the variable expenditures incurred do not exceed $97,000. (Expenditures should receive particular attention, for several of these tasks lie on the critical path and the expenditure to date constitutes the bulk of the total.) Cost overruns at this point are serious, as there is lit-tle possibility of significant savings to come. Analysis of both positive and negative deviations from the amounts allocated to the various cost centers will help improve the cost estimating procedures in the next sea-son.

Network analysis, although powerful, has certain limitations. The most serious is the necessity to determine the relative duration of tasks. If this cannot be done with a reasonable degree of accuracy, task comple-tion dates have little meaning and cannot be used to monitoring progress. This could be ameliorated to some extent by applying PERT, which in-cludes a range of estimates within which the duration is expected to lie.

Even with the use of microcomputers, network analysis is demanding. It is not necessary for activities composed of only a few tasks, or tasks that are not interdependent. It also may not be useful for routine and repeti-tive activities; standard pro forma reporting may well serve their monitoring requirement adequately. In many countries, the use of CPM/PERT is mandatory for contractors who are required to submit detailed implementation schedules with their bids.

4 | Beneficiary Contact Monitoring

BENEFICIARY CONTACT MONITORING is the key to successful overall project monitoring. Physical and financial monitoring—the first main component of a management information system—generally measures a project's provision and delivery of services and inputs. But project managers also need to know whether their services are being accepted and how they are being integrated into, for example, farmers' systems.

As a project is implemented, the perceptions of its intended beneficiaries lead either to a growing demand for its services or to its increasing irrelevance. If the beneficiaries have different motivations than those underpinning the project, it matters little which are more financially sensible. At the very least, satisfactory rates of repeated use of project-supplied inputs let managers know that the project is proceeding steadily. Low rates of repeaters can signal the need for an urgent follow-up study, for there is a chance that the project is based on erroneous assumptions.

Three techniques can be used to keep track of beneficiaries' attitudes and behavior. The first, feasible for credit and similar projects, is to maintain records for each participant and to analyze these periodically to monitor the penetration of the service and the establishment of a clientele. The second is to establish a regular schedule of surveys to enable managers to measure the progress of a project and the responses of its beneficiaries. Formal sampling techniques must be used to get statistically significant data from these surveys. The third technique is to use informal interviews to alert managers to outstanding success stories or problems. Monitoring staff can develop many useful insights by talking to farmers and summarizing their comments. Such interviews can be conducted at project facilities or on the farms. This quick, inexpensive method of sampling users can very effectively capture the atmosphere of a project, even if it does not rely on a representative sample.

The monitoring staff has the primary responsibility for initiating and maintaining contacts with beneficiaries. They must also keep the project records well organized and will usually conduct interviews if sample surveys are needed. (However, sample sizes may be small and questions limited, as discussed later in this chapter.)

The monitoring staff also collates and summarizes the data from physical and financial monitoring, which is often implemented by officers of various project units. The monitoring staff then integrates those data with the information on beneficiaries' responses.

Beneficiary contact monitoring requires that beneficiaries can be identified; this is possible in most agriculture and rural development projects. Project preparation and appraisal reports generally specify intended groups of beneficiaries—whether by location, type of farm, eligibility for services, or willingness to use the project's inputs or techniques—and give working estimates of their number. Example 13 is from a recent appraisal report for a project in which the beneficiaries are well specified and their numbers precisely estimated.

EXAMPLE 13. *The Precise Definition of Beneficiaries*

A statewide agricultural development project in Latin America identified its beneficiaries as rural families living in depressed areas of the state. The guidelines given in the appraisal report for the selection of project areas and beneficiaries state that the project will focus on parcels of less than 50 hectares that are technically and economically suitable for agricultural production and that are occupied primarily by ejidos (communal farmers) and private smallholders. The report estimates the following potential beneficiaries.

* *The beneficiaries are primarily situated in three regions comprising some 317,500 hectares with varying patterns of land tenure. In the coastal plain, central depression, and highlands, about 55 percent of the land is owned by 27,000 ejido families; the remaining 45 percent is owned by about 4,800 private owners. On the coast, ejido holdings average about 8.8 hectares and private holdings 28.6 hectares. In comparison, landholdings in the central depression average 6.8 and 16.2 hectares, respectively. The holdings in the highlands are highly fragmented and range from 0.5 to 3.0 hectares, which leaves more than 80 percent of the population at or below the subsistence level.*

* *Incomes are low; the estimated average annual family income is less than $1,900. About 20 percent of the population is landless and has a high rate of migration within the project regions. The coast is a priority for development because many workers have migrated from other regions to seek regular and seasonal employment. The need for development opportunities is also of concern in the economically depressed highlands; the strong cultural and family ties of that region's 250,000 indigenous people inhibit economic activity or resettlement to other areas of better opportunity.*

- *The project will directly benefit about 32,000 farm families. Its impact will be greatest on the ejidos' holdings that average less than 10 hectares on the coast and 7 hectares in the central depression, as they have the greatest incentives to change production strategies. Farm earnings of direct beneficiaries are expected to increase on average from about $1,900 to $4,800 per family at full development.*

Given such a precise beneficiary specification in the appraisal report, the geographic, holding size, and economic class strata for the monitoring indicators are predefined, as are the target numbers to be reached by the end of the project. The surveys of beneficiaries can be targeted and focused accordingly, which helps considerably in sample selection.

Source: World Bank.

A growing number of projects, however, aim to benefit the farm population in general. For example, a project that calls for fertilizer imports or changes in pricing policy may not specify beneficiaries. Other projects, such as those that support applied agricultural research, cannot predict in detail who will benefit.

Each type of project needs its own schedule for beneficiary monitoring. When beneficiaries are identified in advance, monitoring can start with project implementation. For research projects monitoring starts with farm trials for a selected group of participants. For sector policy projects and structural adjustment investments, monitoring as described in this chapter may not be possible. In such cases, the whole population must be monitored, perhaps the purview of a national ministry or statistics bureau.

Monitoring planners should review project documents to identify the populations that will be directly involved in each stage of the project. Beneficiary contact monitoring can then expand in step with implementation. To summarize the cost benefit streams, project documents may express expected incremental production as an aggregate increase for the entire project area, region, or even nation. This has misled some monitoring systems to monitor the general population with random samples spread throughout the region. But in many such cases, projects start by building infrastructure and supplying services in specific areas and expand these during implementation. Beneficiary contact monitoring should focus on actual contact areas.

What to Ask

Beneficiary contact monitoring should answer the following basic questions:

- Who has access to project services and inputs?
- How do they react to these stimuli?
- How do these stimuli affect their behavior and performance?

The need to elaborate the answers to these questions guides monitoring planners in choosing their methods of obtaining data and in analyzing the responses of beneficiaries.

Management needs to know who is being serviced as implementation gets under way. Is the project reaching its intended clients? Are extension agents serving the targeted deprived farmers or are they diverted to vociferous, more influential farmers? If farm service centers were established to extend supplies of fertilizer and hybrid seeds to a large number of small farmers, who are the clients of these centers? Are they mainly those with transport, contrary to the project's objectives? Are certain groups, such as women farmers, achieving the access accorded their male counterparts?

The monitoring system faces a difficult challenge in determining who *could* have used the services but *chose* not to do so. It is relatively simple to classify the clients of a farm service center. But an extensive survey may be necessary to determine who wants to come but cannot, or who is disinterested despite ease of access. The latter group is particularly important. Their reasons for not using the project's services may be the first pointer to problems that will need further investigation.

The following questions need to be answered in sequence to gauge clients' initial reaction to a project:

- To what extent did persons with access understand the available services?
- To what extent were the services seen as meeting the needs of those who understood them?
- To what extent were the services tried by those who saw them as relevant?
- Did those who tried the services continue using them?

Commercial market researchers use similar questions to monitor the launch of a product. For example, the advertising for a new toilet soap must be tailored to the intended consumer or it might be misinterpreted. The soap might be a more efficient cleanser or have a nice fragrance. But some men might consider the fragrance feminine. And some women might perceive and resent an implication that they are currently not well cleaned. So the first monitoring test determines whether the advertising led to the intended understanding. The product must then meet consumer desires. An expensive perfumed soap could fail if consumers are looking for cheaper soaps. The second test is simple: did consumers try the product? Third, and most important, did consumers transfer brand loyalty, or did they revert to their previous brand?

There are strong parallels between commercial market research and the monitoring of a new hybrid cereal variety or fertilizer. Did the extension service help clients understand the benefits of the new product? Did farmers perceive it as meeting their needs? How many tried it? How many asked for it the following season? And did the demand for it continue when the attention of project staff focuses elsewhere?

These monitoring indicators maintained as a time series are valuable for internal evaluation. Heads of commercial firms stake their future profits on them, but managers of development projects tend not to trust them and instead favor formal evaluations of final economic impact.

The monitoring of the initial effects of a new product on the behavior and performance of farmers extends the monitoring system to one more level of detail—namely the initial outcome of the use of project services in terms of physical output or economic effect. This is a kind of monitoring that shades into what may be called ongoing evaluation for project management. This vital component of the management information system is still, however, essentially the monitoring of project implementation through regular contact with the intended beneficiaries.

This level of monitoring assumes that the farmers, however small and untrained can explain the changes they are making in response to the project and can measure its effects on their productivity. Many development professionals who work with small farmers believe this assumption, and our own experience verifies it. Quantitative reporting by farmers may not be in a standard format but may nevertheless be usable. Moreover, farmers' perceptions are an important part of the management information system. It does not matter whether these perceptions appear logical to project staff or are consistent with objective evidence. Because farmers' attitudes and perceptions are likely to condition their responses, managers need to take them into account in monitoring.

There are two ways to solicit farmers' assessments of project interventions. The first is to get simple feedback from a sample of them on the changes they are making in their farming system and the responses they believe they are getting from inputs. The second (discussed in chapter 5), is to conduct more searching probes of farmers' attitudes, perceptions, and behavior when unexpected responses to the project lead to problems. These problem diagnostic studies are commissioned as required rather then being part of the routine reporting system.

Formal Sampling

Project managers can use sampling as a powerful technique to answer questions about the targeted population without contacting every beneficiary. Regular contacts with beneficiaries to obtain simple indicators, covering their access to services and their adoption of them as part of the monitoring process, are the clearest example of the power of a probability sample; the case for this is made briefly below. (See chapter 6 of the companion volume for a more technical treatment.)

The estimation of a proportion from a small sample of a population has little significance unless it can be used to estimate the proportion for the whole population. Therefore a sample must be drawn in such a way that quantitative inferences about the population can be made. For example, if we interview 100 farmers out of a project population of 1 million, we may find that 20 have adopted the project's recommendation to plant early. But this is of limited interest unless we can infer with a certain confidence that it is likely that 20 percent of the 1 million farmers have adopted this practice.

Sampling theory deals with this need to make quantitative inferences from a sample to a population within a calculable range of error and at a certain level of confidence that the actual proportion, if it were known, would not lie outside this range. The theory requires that every member of the population have a known nonzero probability of selection.

Project officials can define the population to be studied as narrowly as they wish. This allows studies to concentrate only on direct participants in a project. For example, studies could be conducted of farmers who use a project's farm service centers or of farmers who grow particular varieties of crops. A sample to ascertain whether a service such as extension has reached its intended audience, however, will need to be drawn from the entire population, for it is not known in advance which areas have been penetrated and which have not—indeed, the purpose of the sample is to reveal such patterns.

Despite stubbornly held myths, sampling does not have to be complicated, time-consuming, or expensive. The facts are:

- A sample does not necessarily have to be large to meet specified inferential requirements.
- A sample does not depend on the size of the population and therefore does not need to be any particular percentage of it.
- A sample can be drawn from as narrowly defined a group as is desired by project managers and does not have to be drawn from an entire population.
- The size of a sample depends, first, on the variation within a population of the variable being tested (not on the population's size, except in a very limiting case) and, second, on the desired level of confidence that the estimate is within a given margin of the value for the population.

Larger populations thus do not necessarily require larger samples. For example, the sample needed to measure a project adoption rate in India would be about the same as that in Sri Lanka. Failure to understand this is the commonest reason for excessively large samples. Example 14 shows that this error is often made.

EXAMPLE 14. Erroneous Criteria for Determining Sample Sizes

The mistaken belief that the sample size must be a certain percentage of the population is extraordinarily persistent. Consider the following excerpts from recent project appraisal reports which have been approved by national and international authorities.

- *The agricultural planning office would be responsible for overall monitoring of project implementation and for impact evaluation. [The project agency] is instituting a farm recording system on a 10 percent sample of small-scale farmers receiving credit with the technical assistance program. This would facilitate measurement of the impact of the credit program on agricultural production and small-scale farm benefits. An estimated 39,000 farmers are to receive credit, which would result in a sample size of about 4,000.*

- *[The project agency] will monitor the progress of not less than 20 percent of all farm plans in the livestock component and all plans in the poultry component in the course of their implementation.*

- *[The project agency,] with the guidance of the technical specialist on mastitis control, will keep records on at least 20 percent of the herds involved for this purpose of evaluating progress made in controlling the disease.*

- *To allow monitoring and evaluation of the economic effects of project investments, [the project agency] would establish a system satisfactory to [the funding agency] under which technical and financial data would be collected on at least 5 percent of the subborrowers in each category.*

Source: World Bank.

Sampling to estimate the proportion of a population that belongs to one group or another, for example, adopters or nonadopters, benefits from the fact that the required sample size may be quite small if the range of error allowed is a few percentage points. Samples of 100 may suffice for each group for which an independent estimate is required. (This is discussed in detail in chapter 6 of the companion volume.)

For many aspects of beneficiary contact monitoring, simple interviews with a small sample of farmers will provide adequate indicators of project penetration, adoption, and response if the sample is drawn according to randomization procedures. Given the available range of sample designs, it is nearly always possible to do this. We therefore strongly recommend that probability sampling be used in monitoring the proportion of a beneficiary population that exhibits a pertinent characteristic.

Selection of Indicators

Choosing the proper indicators to be measured is crucial to setting up effective beneficiary monitoring. This choice has consequences for the users who will be served, the reporting period, and data collection methods. Inappropriate indicators can doom an information system. Furthermore, failure is sealed when managers choose all the indicators that come to mind or are listed in various guidelines. As the list grows larger, so does the number of inappropriate indicators.

Project managers guide the choice of indicators by deciding what they need to know. Some indicators are especially important because they illuminate matters that the managers can influence to improve project performance. In beneficiary contact monitoring, project managers and the monitoring staff should concentrate on basic data: the number of persons reached by project services or inputs, the number of persons who initially or repeatedly adopt project elements, and the estimated level of production gains that is achieved. These indicators measure physical and behavioral accomplishments and suggest attitudes that determine whether the project will face growing demand or become increasingly irrelevant to farmers' underlying desires.

Once managers have defined the types of indicators, several operational criteria should be applied in choosing the actual indicators. The measurements should be selected with implementation in mind and should be developed according to the basic concepts of speed, regularity, flexibility, and mobility. Criteria for effective indicators include:

- *Unambiguous definition.* The indicator must be clearly defined in the project's context. For example, what is meant by an "adopter" of a project-supplied input such as fertilizer? Does it include all farmers who bought the fertilizer, farmers who apply it but less than recommendations call for, or only farmers who follow the input recommendations? Adoption rates are highly recommended indicators, as discussed below, but they must be clearly defined.
- *Consistency.* The values of the indicators should stay constant as long as they are collected in identical conditions, no matter who does the collecting. As far as possible, indicators should be chosen to give objective rather than subjective data.
- *Specificity.* Indicators should measure specific conditions that the project aims to change. Specificity usually decreases along the path

from inputs, outputs, and effects to impact. For example, the delivery of inputs within a defined area is specific; a changed delivery rate reflects a real change in a project's implementation. Crop output, however, is a less specific indicator, since outside factors may have greater influence on total production than the project. An indicator is especially valuable to project officials if it clarifies possible corrective action.

- *Sensitivity.* Indicators should be highly sensitive to changes in a project situation. For beneficiary contact monitoring, it is especially important that they reveal short-term movements. Indicators that change so slowly that shifts are difficult to detect without a long time series are practically useless for implementation decisions. For example, the managers of a project that provides a new seed to smallholders need to monitor the seed's adoption rate. Short-term movement in this rate in the early years could reveal whether or not farmers favor the seed—a critical monitoring indicator.

- *Ease of data collection.* The collection of the data needed to calculate the chosen indicators should be within the capability of a limited team. The fact that an indicator is believed to be important does not mean that it is practical to measure it.

The choice of basic indicators should be both subsector- and project-specific. What is appropriate for one project is not for another, and what can be measured in one environment cannot be in another. Three principal categories of indicators are described below.

Beneficiary Contact Indicators

Beneficiary indicators illuminate how beneficiaries are exposed and react to project services and inputs. The indicators progress in sequence from measuring the population in general to measuring beneficiaries directly involved in the project:

- What proportion of the target population knows of the project's services or inputs?
- What proportion of the target population has access to particular project services or inputs?
- What proportion of the target population received a particular message, service, or input?
- Of those who received a message, service, or input—who comprise the exposed population—what proportion understood its purpose?
- Of those who received and understood a message, service, or input, what proportion regarded it as potentially helpful?

- What proportion of the exposed population adopted elements of the project for the first time? For example, who followed instructions, bought or applied an input according to recommendations, used a project facility, or borrowed the credit?
- What proportion of the adopting population repeated their use of project services in following seasons in a similar manner or on a similar scale?
- What proportion of the adopting population used project services more intensely in following seasons?
- What proportion of the adopting population continued practices promoted by the project even after the project's facilitating services had been discontinued?
- What is the scaled index of adopter satisfaction—for example, ranging from very disappointed to very satisfied?
- What is the distribution of reasons that potential beneficiaries did not use project services or stopped participating?

Note that the proportions are not always derived from the same population. The number of adopters expressed as a proportion of those who received the message or have easy access to the facility (the exposed population) may be a more meaningful indicator than the number of adopters expressed as a proportion of the target population. If a large part of this population cannot get access to a service, adoption is not possible. There is, however, an interesting exception to this. When an input is available throughout a region and the project is expected to stimulate its usage in a part of it, the comparison of usage rates between project and nonproject areas is an important monitoring indicator.

Movements of these indexes can be compared for different intervals to measure the rate at which the project is moving toward its targets. (The statistical measures to analyze the significance of differences between the values of indexes at different times are described in chapter 9 of the companion volume.)

There are problems in defining adoption. First, if a project recommends a group of combined operations—for example, to plant a certain variety of seed at a certain time and at a certain spacing—is the recipient an adopter if he followed only some of the recommendations? It is possible to consider the recommendations as a set of and to collect figures for each component of the set. Second, if the recommendation is to use X kilos of fertilizer per hectare, is the farmer an adopter if he uses 0.5 X? The answer may depend upon the purpose of the index. Using 0.5 X may represent acceptance of the message and thus indicate effective extension work. If this is what is to be measured, the farmer is classified as an adopter. If the improvement of production is being assessed, however, and 0.5 X is insufficient to affect production, the farmer should not be regarded as an adopter. Example 15 describes adoption rates for a project in India.

EXAMPLE 15. *Measurement of Adoption*

The following adoption criteria were used in a questionnaire survey in India designed to provide the extension service with information on the farmers who applied certain recommendations. A review of how the farmers adopted the recommendations enabled extension efforts to be enhanced or recommendations to be modified. The guidelines used to define adoption are summarized below. They show how somewhat arbitrary dividing lines were of necessity used to classify farmers as adopters, partial adopters, or nonadopters.

Field staff were provided with the list of extension recommendations on which to interview the farmers. The questionnaire, which was intentionally kept short, generally had no more than six questions for each crop. It contained questions on the recommendations of the extension service, what practice the farmer used, the quantity of inputs (such as fertilizer and seeds) used, and the proportion of land on which the recommendation was adopted.

Some recommendations were dichotomous; that is, only a yes or no answer was possible. For instance, did the farmer use the new variety or not? Others, such as recommended rates of application, produced a wide range of responses reflecting usage below (or even sometimes above) the recommended level. For these, a farmer was said to have adopted an input if the amount he used was equivalent to at least two-thirds of the recommended amount. A farmer who used less than two-thirds of that amount was defined as a partial adopter. Nonusage of course defined a nonadopter. A second dimension used to determine adoption levels introduced the amount of land to which the input was applied. The two-thirds rule was used again.

The result of this classification was as follows. For a dichotomous recommendation, full adoption required that an input be used on more than two-thirds of the land. Use on less than two-thirds resulted in a classification of partial adoption. For recommendations on which a more variable usage response was possible, full adoption required that more than two-thirds of the recommended input was applied over more than two-thirds of the land. The intermediate rating of partial adoption was given to farmers who applied the full amount of the recommended input to less than two-thirds of their land or who applied less than two-thirds of the input to some of the land. Nonadoption continued to mean that none of the input was used and therefore that none of the land was involved.

Source: World Bank.

The recording of the data for the calculation of adoption rates does not require detailed questionnaires and lengthy farmer interviews; observation and a few questions will usually suffice. The important conditions for ensuring the maximum effectiveness of these indicators as an important feature of the management information system are the following:

- Speed of data collection and analysis for quick, regular feedback to management
- A well-dispersed probability sample of respondents
- Stratification of the sample to provide estimates for each of the important project zones
- Use of a mobile field force collect data (necessary in the case of a well-dispersed sample)—unless reliance is placed on project staff, such as extension agents.

Output Indicators

Most agriculture and rural development projects aim to increase crop or livestock production as a way to improve farm incomes. It is difficult to measure a project's influence on production changes. A project may actually accelerate an upward movement in production, or at least slow a decline. But complex outside forces acting on the farmer may overwhelm the project's influence; indicators of overall production may not reveal either the direction or size of the project's influence. For example, the use of a project-supplied seed may raise production, but in a drought year this is masked by the drought-induced slump in overall production.

Nevertheless, managers at all levels generally require an indicator of production in the project area. They demand indications of the size of pending harvests or supplies of a commodity to the market. The following indicators provide practical help in meeting this need.

Marketed volume. The volume of commodities passing through selected market outlets can be valuable in two ways: it can be used as a proxy for production movements, and it can guide managers' marketing decisions as an indicator in its own right. In the case of cash crops, measuring the indicator at the "market gate" may be both the simplest and the best method. This is particularly true of crops that pass through tightly restricted marketing channels—cotton, for example, must be sold through a limited and known list of ginneries. In the case of a food crop, much of which is retained for home consumption, interpreting changes in the marketed volume requires an assumption as to how well home consumption needs had been met in earlier seasons. However, managers may actually benefit more by knowing the volume of food crops coming onto the market than by knowing the volume of total production. Managers may not be able to influence farm consumption; it is part of the environment that needs to be recognized. Management decisions may at least influence market share.

Farmer production forecast. Most managers require estimates of the current season's likely production. Farmers in many countries and conditions can reasonably and valuably estimate any changes in their production of a given item by either forecasting the harvest or estimating the amount harvested. The reluctance of monitoring staff in many projects to use farmer estimates is matched only by the staff's ineffective efforts to measure production objectively. The value of farmer estimates—whether forecasts or postharvest indicators of production changes—should not be overlooked.

Trader estimate of supply. Local traders can report seasonal changes in commodity availability. They can develop useful estimates of supply movements through their contacts with both producers and market sellers.

Prices. Local market movements in wholesale prices (whether legally sanctioned or not) can be useful indicators of commodity supplies, especially when interpreted against an existing time series so that normal cyclical movements are discounted.

Explanatory and External Indicators

Managers also need to monitor certain outside forces that a project cannot directly influence but that still affect beneficiaries' behavior and productivity. Such monitoring helps managers factor out these forces so that they can detect the underlying progress of the project. Indicators may be chosen to measure, for example, soil conditions (such as erosion and moisture levels), environmental factors (such as weather), and economic parameters (such as market prices).

Of course, the monitoring of these external indicators may have a more direct role if they reveal that an essential precondition for the success of a project is being removed. An early warning that government pricing policies or inadequacies in an external but essential marketing mechanism are threatening the viability of a project may enable its managers and others to raise policy questions.

Monitoring indicators are also valuable for evaluating a project. Each project is eventually judged by its performance in the context of external forces. For evaluation, high-level managers and external financiers concentrate on such standardized indicators of project performance as crop-specific production increments attributable to the project; the use of project facilities as a proportion of appraisal targets; responses to inputs; social and cultural effects; indicators of undesirable side effects such as pollution, declining nutritional status, and soil erosion; and any positive project impact on incomes and employment. It is often nearly impossible to measure some of these indicators in terms of trends within the projects, but project officials can design some of their monitoring indicators as proxies for them. Moreover, it may be feasible to estimate input responses during project implementation by comparing yields from fields using the input against those from fields without it. Such studies can be undertaken within a single season and are of value to both project managers and evaluators. (These issues are discussed in more detail in chapters 7 and 8.)

5 | *Follow-up Diagnostic Studies for Monitoring*

ONCE THE MAIN COMPONENTS of a monitoring system begin operating properly, the system traces the progress of the project's operations and should reveal problems as they emerge during implementation. The project manager and staff are likely to detect some problems before they are revealed by the information system. But managers may focus on problems occurring at the delivery stage of services and may be slow to sense adverse reactions among the farming population. Monitoring therefore confirms managerial perceptions in some cases and first indicates problems in others. In both circumstances, monitoring needs to take on one additional role: to study problems in order to identify contributing factors so that solutions grounded in empirical data may be proposed.

The monitoring staff must have the ability to carry out ad hoc diagnostic studies and sufficient flexibility in resource allocation to be able to muster the appropriate team. Many projects have had the information that allowed the early identification of problems, but the managers and monitoring staffs of these projects did not recognize the problems because they did not adequately use the information or they did not follow through and conduct a diagnosis to facilitate remedial action. Example 16 shows a case of the omission of such a study in an otherwise fairly comprehensive data set.

EXAMPLE 16. *Failure to Adopt Hybrid Maize*

The main inputs recommended by a rural development project were a hybrid maize seed and fertilizer to use with the seed. Project records provided detailed data on credit issued to farmers' clubs, on the price of seed and fertilizer and the amount sold, and on purchases of the maize crop. The monitoring and evaluation field survey provided annual data from a sample of farmers on the inputs used, the area cultivated under each crop, and estimated yields. Both area and yield data were based on objective measurements.

Review of so-called monitoring and evaluation by supervision missions always concentrated on the farm survey. Even the local monitoring and evaluation officer considered the farm survey output as his product.

As the project neared completion, concern was expressed that the monitoring and evaluation data did not show significant increases in production. The extension staff typically claimed (using their own independent forecasting system) that production had doubled.

The project records showed that, after an early rise funded by credit, sales of the hybrid maize seed and the required fertilizer had fallen off. The farm survey data were entirely consistent with this sequence. Farmers who adopted the hybrid achieved yields double that of local maize, but as the years passed, many of them abandoned it. The data further showed that even the adopters always retained a major part of their cultivated area under local maize. The total production of maize was static because the available area was constrained, and no yield increase had occurred because of loyalty to the local variety, which had attained its yield potential.

The information system therefore contained more than enough evidence to reveal a major problem affecting the project, namely, that farmers were reluctant to switch from local maize to the hybrid, or if they adopted the hybrid they rejected it after one or two seasons.

What was obviously needed was a diagnostic study by a small, experienced team drawn from the project staff to probe the farmers' objections to the hybrid. Various hypotheses were formulated at the time of project completion:

- *The new grain was difficult to pound.*
- *The taste of the local variety was preferred.*
- *The hybrid was viewed as a cash crop by the farmers and had become uncompetitive due to the resulting higher fertilizer prices.*
- *A year of drought had exposed the farmers to credit repayment problems and led to a reluctance to draw credit again.*
- *The hybrid had been changed during project implementation, and the farmers noticed a relative drop in yield.*

These hypotheses could easily have been tested. But no such study had been undertaken for this project, so the diagnosis was uncertain.

Source: World Bank.

Diagnosing and Solving Problems

According to management experts, there are three approaches to problem solving: intuitive, judgmental, and analytical.

Managers who solve problems on the basis of their hunches—their "gut feelings"—are taking an intuitive approach. Intuitive decisionmaking is more widely practiced than is generally recognized. Entrepreneurs often use their intuition to respond to opportunity. Political leaders are guided by intuition in dealing with complex problems. And managers of development projects sometimes must use their intuition in the absence of objective information.

Intuition has serious limitations. Only a few managers have good enough intuition to be consistently successful in solving problems, and there is no way to predict who has such exceptional intuition and who does not. Moreover, intuitive decisionmaking can interfere with the requirement to achieve a coordinated, consensual approach in a project with a complex management structure that involves several agencies.

Managers who base their actions on their subjective experience or knowledge are being judgmental. Managers may try to solve major problems during implementation by depending on solutions that have worked well before. Since many problems tend to be similar, such an approach often succeeds. And the judgmental approach is quick and inexpensive; there is very little need to collect fresh data or hold time-consuming discussions. However, the judgmental approach may let the manager down in unusual cases. Two situations may look similar but have different causes.

The analytical approach gives managers the widest and most reliable range of tools to solve problems. Scientifically valid methods allow them to study problems, understand their causes, and evaluate alternative solutions using well-defined criteria. This method lets managers put their experience into an objective framework in implementing projects. The approach comprises seven analytical steps.

1. *Identify problems.* Define the problem within its context and separate its symptoms from the problem itself. For example, why are farmers not repaying loans or abandoning technical packages after only one trial? Formulate one or more hypotheses about the cause.

2. *Determine contributing factors.* Collect quantitative and qualitative data on suggested causes.

3. *Review constraints on decisionmaking.* Analyze the managers' organizational and political environment for restrictions on their options. Take into consideration such variables as staff composition, morale, and capabilities; political pressures; cultural sensitivities; the good will of the population; and managerial effectiveness. Avoid discussing unrealistic or impractical solutions. For example, project managers might not be able to risk alienating certain groups by taking legal action against some of their members.

4. *Develop alternative solutions.* Use the information from the studies of contributing factors and constraints to formulate a number of realistic solutions—not just the first one proposed.

5. *Appraise possible solutions.* Establish explicit, practical criteria and apply them in examining the advantages and limitations of the major possible solutions.
6. *Recommend the optimal course of action.* Present a ranking of the options and their implications to managers for decision (discussion of which lies outside the present context).
7. *Monitor feedback.* Analyze the effects of the action taken to decide whether further corrections are needed.

These steps are illustrated in figure 4.

Diagnostic Studies Linked to the Monitoring System

Diagnostic studies should be used like surgical tools. They should be specifically aimed at producing empirical information that is useful in solving problems identified by managers with the assistance of the management information system. Consider some simple examples of problems that may occur:

- The targeted population in most of the area covered by the project has accepted an improved variety of maize, but farmers in two districts appear to have rejected it.
- Within a credit project, considerable demand has developed for long-term loans but there is little enthusiasm for short-term ones.
- A record number of farmers joined project-supported farmers' clubs during the first two years of project implementation, but membership is now falling.
- Many farmers initially adopted a new variety of maize, but there are indications that they are reverting to their former variety in succeeding seasons.
- Potable water systems installed by the project stop operating within six months after local groups take over their management.

In each of these cases, a review of the data in the management information system should identify the problem as it emerges and lead to a quick diagnostic study to probe the underlying reasons for these unexpected turns of events. Example 17 shows such a study.

EXAMPLE 17. Diagnostic Study of Tractor Loan Recipients

A national development bank funded a project to promote contract tractor businesses and intensify farm mechanization in the country. The bank offered long- and medium-term loans for the purchase of tractors. As the project expanded, the bank became aware of the increasing number of borrowers who

Figure 4. Steps in Analytical Problem Solving

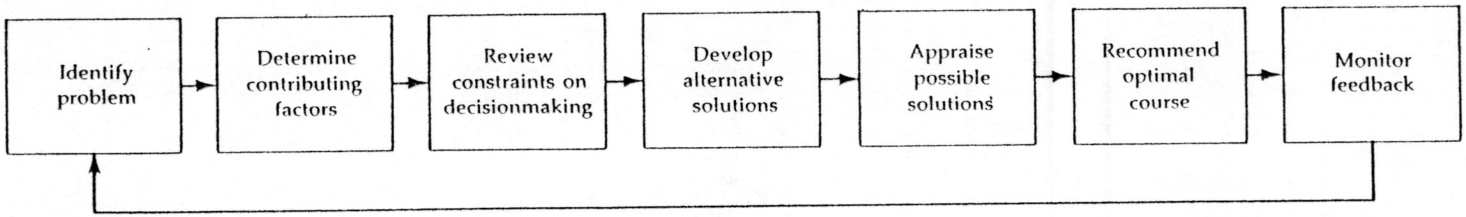

were not meeting repayment schedules and the growing strain placed on its resources by overdue payments.

In view of the potentially severe consequences posed by these overdue loans and defaulters, a diagnostic study was launched to identify the reasons for the high nonrepayment of loans. The first step in the study, which was designed to uncover quickly the reasons for nonpayment, was to review bank records. Borrower profiles were created which included information on occupation, assets, liabilities, and loan status. Defaulting borrowers were then interviewed with a questionnaire. Interviews were also conducted with principal informants— tractor dealers and operators, technicians, officials of the farm research station, credit union staff, bank and ministry officials, and farming experts.

The profiles provided an interesting socioeconomic picture of the borrowers. First, defaulters were the elite of the country—civil servants, traders, private employees, and others. Second, four-fifths of them were not full-time farmers and thus had limited knowledge of farm operations. Third, many had other means of livelihood and were in a position to repay the loans.

In the interviews, it became apparent that most borrowers did not have an accurate idea of the overall costs and had expected an unrealistic return on their investments. The tractor contract business involved a number of hidden costs—for example, problems in hiring untrained drivers, inadequate repair facilities, and a 250 percent increase in tractor insurance premiums in a two-year period.

The study also brought out a number of psychological factors which influenced borrowers' willingness to meet payment schedules. The majority of borrowers were in a position to repay their debts. Because development banks in the country showed little inclination to collect on the defaulted loans, however, agricultural credit was viewed primarily as a source of subsidy to farmers and entrepreneurs.

As a result of the problems identified in the study, the bank made a series of changes. In cases of high unanticipated costs, the bank would now advance additional loans or reschedule the debt if the borrower submitted a viable plan to cover such contingencies. Although it would be virtually impossible to change the psychological perceptions of the borrowers within a short time, new arrangements would be made to encourage borrowers to meet their loan obligations through informal discussions rather than legal action. The bank accepted the study's finding that its own lack of expertise had contributed to the problems of nonpayment and assigned a loan officer to specialize in farm machinery lending.

Source: IFAD.

Diagnostic studies should not be confused with theory-oriented academic research. Confusing them can cause misallocation of resources and delay the process of problem solving. Several monitoring and evaluation units have mistakenly believed that they were helping diagnose problems of project implementation by launching large, time-consuming research studies. These endeavors produced massive sets of data and eventually generated graduate theses and scholarly articles, but they provided little information for timely decisionmaking.

Outside agencies or research organizations may be used to conduct certain studies but should not automatically be chosen to do them. For the same reasons that diagnostic studies should be seen as part of the monitoring function, in most cases they should be done by the monitoring staff.

The characteristics that make ad hoc diagnostic studies quicker and more focused than academic research are outlined in table 3. The following paragraphs discuss the characteristics given in the table.

Audience. A project's managers are the main audience for diagnostic studies. The findings and recommendations presented to them must be brief and clear and should emphasize diagnostic conclusions rather than findings.

Purpose. Decisionmakers need to know the pattern and characteristics of a situation; usually they are not looking for numerical details. The problem has come to light, and a diagnosis of its main causes is needed. It may not matter for a final decision whether the problem affects 65 or 72 percent of the targeted population.

Preferred variables. Diagnostic studies focus on variables that project managers can manipulate. Other variables are treated only marginally or not at all. For example, women farmers might not be using credit. A diagnostic study could focus on lending procedures, the credit staff's attitude toward women, difficulties faced by women in getting agriculture loans, the interest charged, and women's access to the agricultural inputs for which credit is advanced. Project managers can affect these variables. The study would treat only marginally other variables, such as women's low social status, that project managers could do little to change.

Methodology. Because diagnostic studies emphasize speed and flexibility, they collect mainly qualitative information. Various methods of data collection are discussed in the next section.

Quality criteria. Because they must be done quickly, diagnostic studies must relax the standards of theoretical and methodological rigor that normally characterize research. The findings must simply be relevant to the issue and be accurate enough to allow adjustments to implementation procedures to be made with reasonable confidence.

Time frame. Project decisions must be made to fit the deadlines of the working environment. Diagnostic studies must therefore be finished within weeks rather than months if they are going to be useful for decisionmaking.

Applicability. Diagnostic studies aim at particular issues arising from a farmer's reactions to a specific intervention. Even when findings from

Table 3. Distinctions among Diagnostic Studies, Impact Analysis, and Academic Research

				Characteristic			
Type	Audience	Purpose	Preferred variables	Preferred methodology	Quality criteria	Time frame	Applicability
Diagnostic studies	Line managers	Understanding	Manipulable by managers	Mainly qualitative	Sufficient for basis of decision	1–2 months	Specific problems
Impact analysis	National authorities and donor agencies	Verification	Agroeconomic and quality-of-life	Quantitative and evaluative	Some inferential power	Several months or years	Project- or program-specific
Academic research	Academic community	Hypothesis testing and theory construction	Theory derived	Mainly quantitative	Scientific standards	Often extensive	Scientific knowledge

academic research are worded cautiously, they are intended to have a general meaning. And a full impact study sets out to analyze general farmer reaction to the complete range of project recommendations.

Sources of Data

Various data collection techniques can be used to conduct diagnostic studies. They are the subject of the companion volume and therefore are simply outlined here.

Project Records and Documents

Project records and documents can often provide data for diagnostic studies and thus minimize the need for follow-up interviews with the field staff and participants. Records describe the nature, frequency, and effects of events or transactions, although they may not provide deep insight. Documents such as field reports may include quantitative and qualitative data that illuminate participants' motives, beliefs, attitudes, and judgments.

Project records sometimes provide the basis for a diagnostic study using the data on each member of the beneficiary population. For example, the management information system may provide agrodemographic data and a repayment profile for each credit recipient. Analysis of these data may identify factors that affect the likelihood of default.

There are several advantages to using project records and documents: they are available at little or no cost; the project staff can usually identify them easily; inspections do not affect their nature and contents (which is not the case with interview-based surveys); and they provide data that by definition are relevant to the project.

There are also some limitations. First, records and documents are often unrepresentative. This is especially true when not all project units keep comprehensive records; in such cases, variations in the care with which they are maintained may create systematic bias. For example, cooperative societies that perform poorly might also do a poor job of maintaining records. Second, some documents have only questionable validity: project documents often are self-serving. For example, the extension staff can manipulate diaries, records, and other documents to present a promising picture of their efforts and effectiveness. Third, authors may introduce unconscious biases through unexplained gaps that leave researchers free to interpolate their own judgments.

Formal and Informal Surveys

Diagnostic studies can use both formal and informal surveys to gather information. Large-sample surveys are clearly out of the question for studies that need to be completed quickly. But probability sampling can be used if the groups and behavior being studied are narrowly defined and relatively homogeneous, so that the diagnosis can be based on a small sample. In certain instances, purposive sampling is appropriate. This involves the deliberate selection of respondents who exhibit the phenomenon to be studied in a particularly marked way, or who are particularly fluent in articulating the reasons for their behavior that may not have been anticipated by the project plan.

Formal surveys are likely to use standardized questionnaires that are uniformly administered to all the respondents. Such a questionnaire should contain a limited number of simple questions carefully focused on the problem under study. Both closed and open-ended questions may be included; but as one of the main benefits of a standard questionnaire is its suitability for analysis by computer, open-ended questions should be avoided.

Many diagnostic surveys, however, use informal techniques, small, nonrandom samples, and a variety of interviewing or observation modes that do not normally include a standard questionnaire. Informal surveys have several characteristics:

- The project staff, particularly monitoring officers, themselves carry out field interviews to gain firsthand experience; enumerators are not used.
- Interviewers use a checklist, and the resulting semistructured conversations include a free exchange of ideas and information.
- The sampling is flexible. Sample choices are based on judgment or convenience rather than randomization. Also, the sample size is kept very small.
- Investigators use detailed field observation to better understand the context of the issue; for example, a team studying cooperatives would improve its feel for a situation by observing from inside how a typical cooperative works.
- The concepts, hypotheses, and framework for the survey are continually reassessed in the light of the knowledge gained during the investigation.

Informal surveys have the flexibility and potential for speed required by diagnostic studies. They can help provide in-depth understanding of an issue as long as there is no requirement to make inferences for the population about the quantitative incidence of a phenomenon or the average value of a variable. They can be used to disprove a null hypothesis (for example, that a certain constraint does not exist) or to indicate that an assumption of the project plan is not holding true in the cases studied. They are also valuable in ascertaining the attitudes toward and perceptions of the project held by selected individuals or groups.

Informal surveys have limitations over and above their lack of usefulness for making quantitative estimates about the population. A few particularly articulate respondents can make deep impressions and thus distort findings and conclusions. Extreme caution should be exercised in selecting the respondents if randomization principles have not been followed. In addition, there are considerable risks in unstructured conversations of the interviewer (unconsciously) leading the respondent to articulate a perception which in fact is that of the interviewer.

Use of Key Informants

This approach starts from the fact that the status or role of some individuals gives them greater access to information than others. The key-informant approach entails interviewing these knowledgeable individuals for information about others, not about themselves. These informants are chosen according to the information required. For example, while local leaders and extension officials may provide insight about farmers' attitudes toward recommended technical packages, women health workers will know more about the incidence of diseases among women and children. Key informants can be categorized as follows:

- Trained experts, especially those who are active in the project area, such as economists, agricultural scientists, doctors, university professors, and credit experts
- Government officials located in the field, such as the extension staff, health workers, and revenue officials
- Local leaders, such as tribal chiefs, village influentials, and representatives of political parties
- Knowledgeable persons, such as village shopkeepers (with regard to consumption goods) and market traders (about price structures).

Whenever possible, the monitoring staff should draw up an advance list of potential key informants. When they are not familiar with the community being studied, they can start with a few informants and then ask during the interviews for suggestions of additional knowledgeable persons.

The investigator should prepare an advance checklist of issues relevant to the particular informant. The interviewer should also subtly probe the informant during the discussion. In general, however, the informant must be encouraged to lead the interview and thus reveal his views. Interviewers *must* be careful listeners.

Key informants can mislead. Often, they are misinformed or have a distorted perspective. They sometimes deliberately mislead in the hope of benefiting other persons or groups. Examples include village leaders who prematurely conclude that a recommended technical package will not work; extension workers who are convinced their concerted efforts have made a package successful even when the reality is just the opposite; and health workers who seek funding for a new health center by magnifying the incidence of various diseases. This problem can be alleviated by interviewing different categories of key informants to get a balanced picture.

The key informant method works best when interviewers probe for concrete information. This minimizes biases and distortions. For example, more reliable information is obtained by asking a village chief how much land is owned by various households than by asking him a general question about the village's land distribution.

Community Meetings

Community meetings organized at the local level can provide valuable information for diagnostic studies. Such meetings must be carefully planned and organized, with a checklist of issues and questions prepared in advance. The meeting begins with a brief explanation of its purpose; specific questions and issues are introduced gradually. The participants are gently probed for details and explanations, and both their verbal and nonverbal behavior are carefully observed and recorded. Large groups are not conducive to the free exchange of ideas. Participants should be divided into groups of no more than about thirty persons.

The main advantage of community meetings is that they are economical and can be easily arranged. They have succeeded in rural settings because people know each other and are reasonably familiar with what goes on in the community. Moreover, many societies traditionally hold community meetings on important occasions or subjects, so participants feel quite at ease in such a setting.

Project managers and monitoring staff must also remember the limitations of community meetings. A few persons, generally leaders or those with relatively high social or economic status, tend to dominate discussions. They try to answer questions on behalf of the "silent majority." It is often difficult to restrain them without seeming offensive. Furthermore, community members may be reluctant to make critical remarks which might antagonize project authorities or government officials.

Community meetings can also be manipulated. Local organizers may conveniently forget to invite "troublesome" beneficiaries. They may "suggest" to a few participants that a particular point of view should be presented or opposed. Such manipulations can undermine spontaneous discussions and prevent objective information from being gathered. Those conducting the inquiry should watch for such manipulations and correct the situation by gentle probing and cross-checking.

It may be necessary to meet separately with different categories of beneficiaries. For example, separate sessions may be needed for female and male farmers if the women would be reluctant to differ openly with their male counterparts in their presence. In such cases, a preliminary group meeting has led to follow-up interviews with selected individuals who attended the meeting. Such a combination can be effective, particularly because a reaction at the group meeting helps to identify those who have clearly held views on the issues and represent the main bodies of opinion.

Participant Observation

Participant observation can give project managers an in-depth view of a community's attitudes and behavior that they cannot get from superficial encounters between interviewers and respondents. This technique places observers in a community for a long term so that they can have an insider's perspective but maintain an outsider's objectivity. The observers cultivate trust and encourage community members to talk openly by participating in ordinary activities. The method facilitates acceptance in many rural societies whose attitudes range from close identification with near relatives and neighbors to a wary distancing from such outsiders as the extension staff.

A participant observation study takes a long time. It takes time to become an insider and gain the necessary depth of understanding. Moreover, monitoring and evaluation staff members may need on-site training to undertake such studies. The method therefore may not be feasible for diagnosing problems that have to be solved quickly. But projects that extend over several years can begin participant observation early in implementation; the effort might reveal the initial emergence of unexpected reactions that otherwise would be detected only when implementation is adversely affected. Potential opportunities, as well as problems and remedies, may also be identified. Furthermore, opportunities may exist to use quicker direct observation techniques. Short stays in a project locality may be sufficient to achieve many of the insights expected from a full participant observer. (These options are discussed in chapter 4 of the companion volume.)

Planning a Diagnostic Study

Diagnostic studies are triggered when the project staff or the information system reveals that the intended beneficiaries have unexpected reactions to services or inputs. Once the staff has suggested explanations for the situation, the managers direct the monitoring staff to do a quick diagnostic study. This staff then follows the same basic steps used to establish the data and sources required for the regular information system—but faster, with a sharper focus and an emphasis on pragmatic solutions.

The manager must engage in a dialog with the monitoring staff in order to define precisely the problem to be studied and to share any background information on the situation. A dialog is also needed in order to balance the manager's need for information and the monitoring staff's ability to deliver it on time with the available resources. At this stage it is necessary to make a list of possible remedies to the problem that can be explored during the study.

Once this dialog has been completed, the monitoring staff designs and executes the study in the agreed time. The survey must be as rigorous as is allowed by this imperative need to complete the study on schedule.

The acceptance of a study's findings and recommendations depends on the credibility of the collected information in decisionmakers' minds. The monitoring staff must answer to their own satisfaction the following questions in order to assess the technical feasibility of meeting the manager's expectations:

- Which groups in the population should be contacted for the information needed to diagnose the problem?
- Are quantitative or qualitative or both types of data needed?
- What level of precision and confidence is required in formulating the diagnosis and recommendations for action?
- What questions can be answered on the basis of data that can be practically assembled in the allotted time?

To select the suitable method for data collection, the following questions need to be considered:

- Which collection methods can provide the needed data in the allotted time?
- Will the adoption of more than one method provide an opportunity for cross-checking the findings or only result in conflicting and incompatible data?
- What are the skills of those who will conduct the study in the field?
- What budget and logistical support can be supplied to the field operations?

The data analysis should be as simple as possible. Simple descriptive statistics may be just as illuminating as complex tabulations. The monitoring staff should decide before fieldwork begins how the data will be processed. In too many cases a good job of collecting relevant data is performed, not followed by a good analysis to elicit the findings of relevance to the decisionmakers. Study designers should include the following considerations in their planning:

- Does the project have the required filing and processing facilities to deal with the expected volume of quantitative or qualitative data?
- How will qualitative data be recorded and analyzed?
- If the study uses checklists and open-ended interviews, how will the team translate its impressions into a report?

The monitoring staff must consider the opportunity costs of any proposed study. Expenses should be minimized by focusing studies on the manager's main concerns, by using the simplest, cheapest methods to collect data of merely adequate precision, and by collecting the minimum of data needed to fill existing gaps. Once the study plan has been outlined and the costs determined, the designers and project managers should be sure that the study will produce information that is worth as much or more than the cost of collecting it.

The monitoring staff should be prepared to estimate for project managers the comparative costs and risks of conducting the study and finding a potential solution to a problem, or of misdiagnosing the problem if no study is conducted, or of conducting the study and failing to produce a diagnosis that suggests a solution. Both managers and monitoring officials should keep cost considerations in perspective. Many agriculture and rural development projects provide millions of dollars of inputs and services; a simple diagnostic study might cost a few thousand dollars. When unexpected beneficiary responses threaten a project, it would be shortsighted to proceed with implementation without investing in an attempt to find out from the participants themselves what is causing the problem.

While no formulas are available to determine precisely the costs and benefits of a study, the discussions suggested here attune both managers and monitoring staff to balancing costs and benefits. Ultimately, the managers must decide whether it is worth actually authorizing the proposed diagnostic study.

The managers and the monitoring staff should agree before the study begins on when and in what form the results will be reported. Diagnostic study results should be succinct, focused on the problem, and designed to help managers make decisions. They should not be progress reports or academic papers. Too many projects are wrongly preoccupied in their daily operations with formal, lengthy reports. (The next chapter considers the question of communicating information in the general context of monitoring.)

These questions need to be considered in planning a diagnostic study:

1. Who suggested the problem?
2. What is the problem?
3. What are the possible causes of the problem?

4. What type of data and information are needed?
5. How will the desired data be gathered?
6. How will the data be analyzed?
7. How will the findings and recommendations be used?
8. How much time is required to complete the study?
9. What will the study cost?
10. Are there major constraints that can affect completion of the study?
11. What local individuals and agencies might be helpful in conducting the study?

The findings of a diagnostic study may have implications for changes to the project that go beyond the manager's authority. In such a case the manager must communicate with central authorities, for a major interim evaluation of the project may be required. This possible development is picked up in chapter 7 in the context of interim and midterm evaluations.

6 | Communicating Information

ONE OF THE GREATEST WEAKNESSES of management information systems has been the lack of effective and timely communication of information to their users. A monitoring staff often invests much time and many resources to meticulously gather potentially significant data, but they also frequently fail to interpret and present the data in a form that will convey their meaning to managers and other concerned persons. In such cases the monitoring staff may simply give interested parties a bulky, laboriously prepared report which conceals rather than reveals its main message. Such a view of the monitoring role is shortsighted and self-defeating. A principal part of the monitoring function is to convey messages so that they can be easily understood. Proper actions by decisionmakers may not always result from understanding but are precluded without it.

This chapter focuses on how to identify and communicate relevant information. We begin by identifying the kinds of information that need to be communicated and then discuss the various modes of communication—written reports and briefs, oral presentations, and visual displays. Finally, we briefly mention the nature of utilization. We confine ourselves to the communication of monitoring information (including diagnostic studies) and do not cover impact evaluation studies.

Findings, Interpretations, and Recommendations

There are clear distinctions among the findings revealed by the data in a management information system, the logical interpretations that follow from these findings, and recommendations for action. The findings indicate empirical (often statistical) results; they constitute the basic presentation of the salient facts in the data set. For example, the fact that 40 percent of the small farmers in the project area have joined farmers' clubs in order to procure fertilizers and an improved variety of seeds is a finding. When we explore the issue of why only 40 percent have joined the clubs, however, we move beyond the realm of findings and commence interpretation. Obviously, there can be several interpretations: there is a shortage of club organizers, or they have failed to reach particular groups of farmers, such as women, who constitute a significant proportion of the farming population. Interpretations are grounded in empirical evidence but require certain deductions to be made based on this evidence. Confidence in these interpretations will depend on the validity of the data set and the deductive ability of the interpreter. If formal statistical analysis is possible, the confidence levels can be calculated, but in many cases this will be neither possible nor necessary. Sometimes, interpretations are based on plausible but untested hypotheses, which must be so labeled. Recommendations consist of proposed courses of action based on interpretations of the findings.[1] An example of a possible recommendation is that more women extension workers should be recruited to organize womens' clubs.

In order to interpret and recommend, it is essential that the statistical findings first be compiled cogently into tables. This is a direct, minimal responsibility of the monitoring staff, but one that is often badly carried out. Data from the management information system are compiled on a computer and printed out in bulky tables, often with identifications and row and column headings that can be understood only by the authors of the computer programs. The task of the monitoring staff is to

- *Reduce* this mass of detail into clearly labeled simple tables and eliminate unnecessary cells and digits
- *Integrate* the resulting tabular output from various components of the information system; for example, link input supply data with farmer utilization data
- *Assemble* the results over time or by geographical area, as appropriate, so that trends and interarea comparisons are revealed.

Much can be achieved by calculating simple rates and averages, ranking items, and constructing simple summary tables. Exploratory analysis of this kind is an essential feature of monitoring, even if more complex analyses are needed at a later stage. Once the data have been thus marshaled, reduced, and assembled in an appropriate format, the salient findings can be set down. This requires the basic skill of reviewing a table and identifying the story it has to tell. Without this skill, the remainder of

---

1. Michael R. Patton has proposed an additional category of making judgments. According to him, interpretations involve deciding what data mean and determining the significance of the findings. Judgments, in contrast, involve bringing values to bear in such a way that the managers can decide if the findings indicate something positive or negative, good or bad. See Michael R. Patton, *Practical Evaluation* (Beverly Hills, Calif.: Sage, 1982), pp. 272–75.

the process of interpreting and identifying recommendations becomes meaningless.

As indicated above, interpreting the findings may require familiarity with more formal analytical tools. Even here, however, much can be achieved by the use of simple ranked indexes of performance relative to targets, simple graphic display of the data over time, cross tables and the resulting comparisons of proportions, and simple standardization and correlation techniques. Each case needs to be considered on its merits, but the following guidelines are offered:

- The "tabulate everything against everything" attitude should be avoided at all costs.
- The sensitivity of the findings to data inaccuracies should be tested by simulating alternative data sets.
- Sophisticated methods are often useful, but the results must be interpreted with great care.
- Statistical significance does not necessarily imply substantive significance.
- Conversely, the lack of statistical significance in tests using demanding levels of confidence does not mean that the differences are of no interest or are unimportant.

(The methods and approaches to identification of the findings and interpretation of the meaning are dealt with in more detail in chapters 9 and 10 of the companion book.)

Even when the findings and interpretations are adequately presented, the development of recommendations is often either omitted by the monitoring staff or tackled weakly. Sometimes this is the result of inadequate consideration of the need to generate recommendations; they are regarded as afterthoughts when a report is already prepared. But sometimes it is because the monitoring staff believes that to carry the information through to the stage of preparing recommendations is beyond its responsibility. Indeed, many managers instill this belief because of their own attitude toward monitoring. Resolution of this problem requires that the principles offered in chapter 1 be applied. As managers develop their relationship with the monitoring staff, the staff's responsibilities should come to be seen as logically culminating in identifying problems that require urgent action or at least in giving the managers options for their consideration. Experienced managers recognize that there are several alternative courses of action that can be followed in a given instance, and the presentation of these alternatives indicates to the decisionmakers that the monitoring staff is realistic in its assessment and does not presume to make the judgments that are the responsibility of higher authorities.

Style of Presentation

In the next section, we consider the advantages and disadvantages of the various modes of communication. But whatever mode is chosen, certain principles must be followed in order to improve the chances that the information will be received, understood, and acted upon. These principles include:

- A presentation designed for the targeted audience
- Timeliness
- Credibility of material presented
- Brevity and clarity.

In preparing a presentation, in whatever format, it is important to keep in mind the question, "To whom is the material addressed?" The recipients of monitoring information can include

- Beneficiary groups
- Project field staff
- Institutional managers in cooperatives or the private sector
- Project managers
- Local government officials
- An interagency coordinating committee
- Elected or appointed local leaders
- Sectoral planners
- National ministries and financing agencies.

The interests and concerns of these recipients are not necessarily identical. Each of them is concerned with a particular kind of responsibility. For instance, in an area development project, the credit manager will be vitally interested in the progress of the credit component but less so in the construction of health centers. Therefore, the information should be targeted to meet the distinctive needs of the specific audience. This will often involve separate presentations for different audiences. Each report might provide detailed information about a specific component or topic but only a very brief summary of items concerning other components.

Timeliness has been stressed at several points in the earlier chapters. Its importance is so obvious, especially for the communication of findings, that it seems banal to stress it again. Unfortunately, however, although uncontested in principle, timeliness is not frequently practiced. Precise agreement between information users and the monitoring staff on the agreed frequency of communication is the key to successful information transmittal. Certain principal decisions take place on known dates, so not only the timing but also the content of reports can be coordinated accordingly. The most informative report is useless if the decision to which it should have contributed has of necessity already been made. The frequent inability of project managers to rely on their monitoring staff is often caused by a lack of confidence that the information required will be available when it is needed.

Late information may be the result of late identification of the need to collect data on the topic in question, a data collection method that requires a lengthy survey and period of analysis that extend beyond the deadline, or an impression by the monitoring staff that decisions are made on the basis of other sources of evidence and that monitoring reports are only for the record. If the procedures for designing a management information system presented in the earlier chapters are followed, these traps can be avoided. Some progress reports called for in the project documentation are intended as a means of building up the historical records of the project, but the monitoring staff should focus primarily on providing timely information of more direct relevance to decisions on implementation. In presenting recommendations, a clear distinction should be made between core and peripheral recommendations. The former deal directly with the central question, whereas the latter deal with secondary issues that emerged in the course of the study or in the analysis of the data.

The credibility of the findings and of the interpretations based on them is very important. To be acceptable to the decisionmakers, the findings should either be consistent with their own impressions and frame of reference or be based on such solid evidence that these mistaken impressions are overcome. The monitoring staff's fate is often as follows: if the information confirms the manager's preconceived impressions, the staff is told "I knew that already"; if the information is contradictory to such impressions, the staff is disbelieved.

Project managers receive information from various sources, and the formal submissions presented by monitoring staff may follow rather than precede the others. For example, a survey might find that the majority of the farmers who had accepted the technical package has now discarded it. It is quite likely that the manager is already uncomfortably aware of this disturbing fact from his personal contacts with the extension staff or from the sales records for seeds and fertilizers. One implication of this is that compiling and summarizing such data as sales records is part of monitoring. The survey should merely confirm a phenomenon already communicated by the monitoring staff using the management information system. The other implication is that the monitoring presentations should provide a more solid basis for the manager's impressions, which reassures him that they are correct.

The greater problem comes when the monitoring data go against the current assumptions on which the manager is basing his actions, especially when such evidence shows that the project is not progressing as well as was hoped. Historically, the bearers of bad news are not popular, and the monitoring staff will be no exception. In such cases, it is important that the presentation be objective, frank, constructive, and sympathetic in tone. The limitations of the data and findings should be explicitly stated. These limitations may include imprecise conceptualization, limited resources and tools for data collection, gaps in the gathered data, and of course interpretation based on plausible inferences rather than statistical rigor. A little candor only adds to the credibility of the report, as long as the author himself believes the essential findings, even after allowing for these limitations. If the monitoring staff does not believe its own evidence, it should not present it; the staff should instead seek urgent confirmation or rebuttal by other means.

Of course, credibility, like beauty, is in the eye of the beholder. Many monitoring units consist of junior, inexperienced staff who are unable to make their case forcefully in the presence of senior managers. In such a circumstance, the case, even if based on solid evidence, is not taken seriously. Example 18 is taken from a midterm review of a monitoring and evaluation system. A report was submitted that had far-reaching implications but which resulted in no action because nobody believed it—including the authors.

EXAMPLE 18. Lack of Credibility in a Survey Report

In a large African rural development project, the report of an annual survey told project managers the unlikely story that the use of fertilizer had resulted in a decline in crop yields. These unexpected findings, which challenged the very rationale of the project, did not cause a single detectable ripple of reaction among the managers or the evaluation agency that had compiled the data.

Fertilizer response tables showed that only sorghum responded positively; other crops, including maize, had an unlikely negative response to fertilizer. It might have been expected that interviews would have been conducted on a subsample of farmers used in the survey to ascertain whether these results were plausible. Another option would have been for the project staff and the evaluation agency to meet and discuss the implications of the findings.

But, over the years, the project staff had disregarded the reports as often inaccurate and of generally little consequence to project activities. Even the evaluation agency was skeptical of the statistics they had compiled. Thus no attempt was made at either level to review the data critically. The report's unusual findings went unchallenged and were even incorporated into a larger data set to produce aggregate production figures for the region comprising the project area.

When for the latter purpose the data underwent editing checks and adjustments for entry into a computer system, it became evident that the findings were in error. Very different results were obtained which showed a positive response to fertilizer for all crops. But no specific printout was produced to amend the earlier report, and the managers were not informed of the new findings. Only when a supervision mission challenged the credibility of the initial report were these discrepancies brought to light.

The report's conclusions were largely attributed to enumerator biases in data collection and coding errors in processing. Had the evaluation agency critically reviewed the data before issuing the report, most of these errors would have been detected. The indifference shown by the agency in issuing reports in which it had no faith and its reluctance to correct the information were matched by the managers' failure to question the findings.

Source: World Bank.

Brevity and clarity of presentation are important aids to information transfer. In the next section, the importance of routine short briefing reports is stressed. In general, the compilation of lengthy progress reports has led to an impression that comprehensiveness is more important than clear communication of the essential facts. Most routine presentations should be succinct, shorn of circumlocution and evasion. If written, reports should not normally exceed twenty pages, and even then begin with a one- or two-page summary of the findings. When the reader understands the significance of the findings, he may call for a more detailed set of documentation. For this reason, the full documentation should be maintained in a format suitable for circulation.

Clarity must accompany brevity if the desired result is to be achieved. Material often is presented in such a turgid and confused way—without any attempt to marshal the facts and make interpretations—that it makes no impact on the recipient. Communications that are not understood are no better than no communication. If brevity is the soul of understanding, clarity is its heart. Example 19 shows the responses of various users to three types of monitoring and evaluation presentations.

EXAMPLE 19. *Responses to Three Types of Reports*

At a regional workshop in Africa on monitoring and evaluation systems, the speakers stressed the importance of communicating monitoring and evaluation results in a way that could be readily understood and used. They also emphasized the need for brevity, recommending that two- or three-page, issue- or problem-oriented summaries be prepared and that full evaluation reports be used basically as source documents.

During the workshop, one speaker presented a review of responses to three types of evaluation reports: a comprehensive report of about fifty pages, a preliminary field manager's report of three to four pages, and a briefing memorandum of two to three pages that focused on project-specific issues.

Respondents included the project field staff, project managers, and government policymakers and consultants. The tabulated responses showed that the briefing memorandum gained the widest exposure and provided the most assistance to the field staff, managers, donor agencies, and policymakers. The main users of the comprehensive report were consultants and researchers, which suggests its limited use in meeting other respondents' needs. The preliminary report was well received by the field staff and project managers.

Source: World Bank.

Modes of Communication

Outputs from the management information system can be communicated in various ways, including written reports, verbal presentations, and visual displays. The emphasis in most projects is on written reports, to the virtual exclusion of the others. But even when written reports are necessary, verbal presentations are essential, for, as one author puts it, "real communication, insofar as the manager is concerned, will be verbal." Visual displays also can sometimes convey a message more effectively than the written or spoken word.

Written Reports

There are three distinct types of written monitoring reports: formal progress reports, special reports based on problem diagnostic studies, and informal briefs to managers in the form of memorandums or short papers that highlight a current issue.

FORMAL PROGRESS REPORTS. Progress reports are usually done with a standard format. The obvious advantage of this is that, since all the items are specified, no relevant item is overlooked. The standard format also enables managers to make comparisons quickly over time. But excessive standardization can inhibit the reporting of unexpected events and occurrences that do not fit the preconceived categories. Although certain categories of reports, particularly those concerning physical and financial monitoring, should be standardized, sufficient latitude should be provided to allow special treatment and formatting of such categories as beneficiary responses and the emerging effects of project interventions.

Kettering and Schmidt suggest the following framework for monitoring progress with periodic reports:[2]

1. Data about the intended accomplishments, are compared with
2. data of actual accomplishments, to identify
3. significant deviations from plans, as a basis for
4. problem identification and opportunity analysis, to identify
5. corrective action, alternatives, and achievements.

This framework can be applied for each accomplishment, including physical infrastructure, work levels, costs, input supply, resource utilization, target group coverage, and even beneficiary response.

Progress reports should contain different levels of detail according to the management level addressed—that is, the strategic, implementation, or activity level. At the strategic level, many details about implementation progress for each activity are not necessary. What is mainly required is a general review of the project's progress and problems. The focus of monitoring for this level thus is on the principal elements of project performance, indicators of overall achievements, and specification of the problems encountered. More detailed information is needed at the implementation level; its purpose is to facilitate day-to-day overall project management. The information should help managers coordinate and supervise various activities and set new targets. Progress reports prepared for the project staff in charge of a specific activity need to include still more information on that activity. Such reports are usually prepared jointly by the monitoring and field staffs. Finally, how the report is distributed within the management hierarchy can be crucial in getting remedial action taken. A system should be developed to ensure that the various levels of management receive relevant reports in time.

In summary, progress reports are submitted at an agreed frequency, usually quarterly or semi-annually. However, the principal activities during the implementation of an agriculture project are not evenly paced. Thus a quarterly interval is too infrequent for project managers during peak agricultural periods, whereas such a report may contain redundant information during slack periods. Hence, either the periodicity of reporting should be variable or the reports should be briefer for slacker periods. Coverage should include the following topics, albeit briefly:

2. Merlyn H. Kettering and Terry D. Schmidt, *Improving Project Monitoring and Implementation Systems: A Strategy and Implementation Plan for a Project Information System (PMIS) for USAID/Thailand* (Washington, D.C.: U.S. Department of Agriculture Development Project Management Center, 1981).

- The current status of the project
- The major activities undertaken during the period under review (tasks completed or in progress within each activity), cross-referenced to agreed work plans
- The project cost performance
- The estimates of the number of beneficiaries serviced, relative to targets, and their responses
- The current and potential problems (this includes description of the problems and remedial actions planned or recommended)
- The project plans and schedules for major activities during the next review period.

PROBLEM DIAGNOSTIC REPORTS. Unlike progress reports, problem diagnostic reports based on field studies are focused on a limited, specific issue; their purpose is to explore a problem in depth and to make viable, practical recommendations. Their content will vary according to the problem and the chosen mode of study, but they should be as brief and free from jargon as possible. Such reports can include:

- A short statement defining the problem and the history of its identification
- A description of its underlying causes and context
- An assessment of how the problem is affecting project implementation
- A discussion of the possible courses of action, if possible with an indication of the recommended course.

MONITORING BRIEFS. A brief is a written, condensed statement that provides relevant and important information in a format suitable for immediate communication. It is often derived from a comprehensive document or set of records which already exist, although it is not necessarily in a readily accessible form. The most common formats for such briefs are informal memorandums and somewhat more formal executive summaries.

Memos are perhaps the most versatile medium for conveying written results and recommendations. Their format, layout, and content can be designed to increase visual impact and heighten the interest of the recipient. One simple example is the preparation of a single-page memo attached to the top of a document. In a workshop held in Botswana in 1984, a monitoring and evaluation officer reported that although his surveys showed that the application of fertilizer was making no difference to average maize yields, project managers took no notice of this important finding. The survey reports had been routinely submitted to the manager but in all probability had not been read. Had he sent a half-page memo along with the routine reports that clearly stated his finding and its implications, the manager probably would have taken serious notice of it. Although there still might have been no resulting action, this would have been a deliberate decision rather than a failure to appreciate the situation. Moreover, a memo addressed to an individual by name cannot be brushed off as easily as an impersonal report. A memo can range up to a couple of pages, but the briefer the better.

Summaries of academic reports, often affixed at the end of a study, provide a succinct view of the findings, the problem investigated, the underlying hypotheses, and the research methodology used. This is not the recommended format for reports to managers. First, summaries at the end of a document do not easily catch the reader's attention. Second, such summaries tend to provide more detail than is required by decisionmakers. For instance, a project manager may not be concerned with the methodology used to gather the data for an investigation of a credit disbursement problem; he is interested in the dimensions of the problem itself.

Our recommendation, therefore, is to provide what is termed an executive summary. This has two distinct features: placement and selectivity. An executive summary immediately follows the title page or at least precedes the table of contents. It is not designed to summarize the whole report; it covers only, and thereby stresses, those elements which are of direct and immediate relevance to the decisions that the managers face. An executive summary can be structured as a succinct, continuous text or as an itemized list of major points (possibly cross-referenced to the main text).

An interesting way to present a brief is in the form of questions and answers. Here is a hypothetical example of the findings of a monitoring survey:

QUESTION: What percentage of the farmers have adopted the recommended variety of maize seed?

ANSWER: Approximately 30 percent of farmers used the recommended variety during the last season. This is close to the targeted figure, so in terms of adoption the project is on schedule.

QUESTION: What percentage of the farmers who used the improved variety this season also used it previously?

ANSWER: More than 90 percent of the farmers who used the new variety had used it previously and expressed satisfaction with it. Of the nonusers, however, only a negligible number have tried it previously. It would appear that emphasis is needed on promoting initial adoption.

QUESTION: What is the percentage of women farmers using the recommended variety?

ANSWER: The sample of women farmers was small, but very few of them had tried the new variety, and most were unaware of it. It may be that the extension effort is not reaching women.

And so on. This question-answer format appears simplistic and certainly elementary. It emphasizes a point by indicating the type of question that it serves to answer. There is a danger that the reader may infer that he is incapable of realizing the significance of the finding without such assistance. But it can be useful in conveying pertinent information to those who lack the expertise to draw the required inferences from detailed statistical findings. It is surprising how commonly even professionals are unable to digest a series of numbers and percentages. The use of the question-answer format is quite common in the fields of health and education. There seems no reason why it may not be used, on occasion, in agriculture.

Briefs should be treated as supplements to, not substitutes for, well-written, comprehensive reports. Their purpose is to attract the attention of the concerned decisionmaker to lead him to pursue the matter further in the full report. A simple listing of findings tends to oversimplify the situation, particularly if complex interrelationships are involved. Often, too, the monitoring system is under pressure to present a more optimistic picture than the data warrant, and briefs may unintentionally serve this purpose.

Verbal Communication

Verbal communication is probably the most effective mode of communication. Evaluation studies of how decisions are made by managers and planners show that much of the information used in reviewing options is obtained through personal contacts and oral presentations.

One advantage of verbal communication is that it is quick; it takes less time to speak than to write the words on paper. Moreover, the presentation can be adapted to the concerns and questions of the audience as the meeting progresses. The direct feedback from the audience, whether one or many, whether by verbal or facial reaction, helps the presenter avoid misunderstandings that could undermine the credibility of the results.

Oral presentations can be made either in individual meetings with project managers or in group meetings with concerned officials or beneficiaries. Both types have their advantages and limitations.

Individual meetings in a sense are confidential, even if not expressly designated as such. Sensitive or critical information can be conveyed better in individual than in group meetings. Many managers feel threatened when critical information is conveyed to them in writing or is shared with a wider audience. There is a great advantage to be gained by the monitoring officer if he has ready access to the project manager. (Often, much can be communicated by making a telephone call or dropping into someone's office to alert him to a potential problem.) Regrettably, all too often, such one-to-one access does not exist.

Group meetings—staff meetings, community meetings, seminars, and symposiums—are useful when the monitoring outputs are of interest to a wider audience. Such meetings do not have to be called specifically to discuss such outputs. Monitoring findings can be shared in meetings organized for other purposes. For example, the monitoring staff can make useful contributions in a meeting of the extension staff by drawing on information in the management information system with which the other staff is not familiar.

Group meetings are a particularly useful format for conveying relevant findings and recommendations to project beneficiaries. In these meetings they can get information, articulate their perspective, and make useful recommendations. Such feedback to the monitoring staff is itself an important source of information that may further improve the quality of findings.

Public meetings should be carefully planned to take account of the interests and the composition of the audience. Several questions should be considered in advance: What information should be presented? Is the information to be presented of interest to all the members of the audience? How much detail is required? It is always preferable to prepare the outline of a presentation in advance but to retain flexibility to allow for any diversions when questions are asked.

Visual Displays

Visual displays are generally used to illustrate the data in reports or oral presentations. But in many instances they can be independently utilized to convey the message without any text. Consider, for example, the rates of adoption by farmers of a recommended package over the years of the project. A simple graph depicting the rise in these rates can effectively convey the message. Such a graph maintained and updated regularly on the wall of a project manager's office can be a powerful monitoring tool.

Of all the visual displays in monitoring reports, tables are most widely used. Too often, however, they are so badly constructed that their message is hidden. There are universally recognized conventions for preparing tables. Essentially, numbers should be rounded to the nearest hundred or thousand units or converted to percentages and simple distribution parameters so as to reveal the table's significant story. (Some tables may be included to complete the record, even though no significant feature emerges; these should be tucked away in annexes to the main report.)

Graphs usually are more effective in capturing the reader's attention than tables. All kinds of graphs, particularly pie chart, bar, and line, can be used for monitoring purposes; example 20 illustrates these. Since readers have a tendency to look at graphs without reading the surrounding text, every graph given in a report should be self-explanatory with a complete title, full labeling, and a key to symbols. When necessary, footnotes about the nature of the data used can be added.

EXAMPLE 20. Simple Examples of Visual Displays

Pie charts show what proportion of the whole each category occupies. They are simple nontechnical displays; see figure 5. Their main limitation is that they are not suitable for comparison with other types of graphs.

Bar graphs convey an immediate impression for comparison along a single axis and can also give a limited subdivision through the use of shading; see figure 6.

Line graphs are used to show trends and can reveal major departures from the trend. They should be kept simple, as in figure 7, although a limited number of comparative trend lines can be superimposed on the same graph.

Distribution maps use a marker to indicate relative concentrations of a variable according to geographic location and thus show patterns at a glance; see figure 8.

Maps also come under the category of visual displays. Complicated geographic patterns of data, although difficult to describe verbally or in writing, can be readily understood when presented as a map. Maps can be used to describe the location of various delivery systems built by a project or beneficiary response rates in various areas. For example, suppose a project has established 200 farmers' clubs in twelve districts of a province covered by the project. Locating these clubs on a map can provide an interesting overall picture. It shows areas of concentration, which districts are well served, and which are relatively untouched. Moreover, if the map is compared with knowledge of the area and its population, hypotheses can be generated that merit further investigation. Valuable information can be conveyed even if the maps are not expertly drawn or very precise.

Finally, Gantt charts and performance networks can be mentioned in this context. They facilitate the use of the management information system in planning work schedules and future programs, and in measuring performance against planned targets. (A description of their use was given in chapter 3.)

Figure 5. Credit Recipients by Percentage of Land Tenure

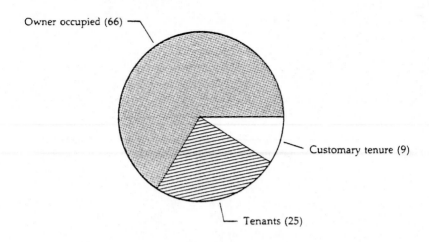

Figure 6. Credit Recipients by Year

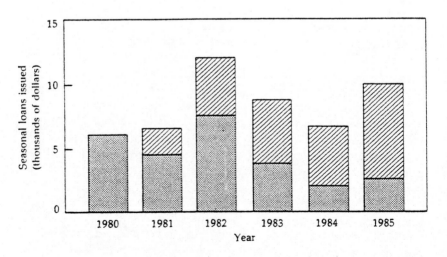

Figure 7. Sales of Maize by Credit Recipients

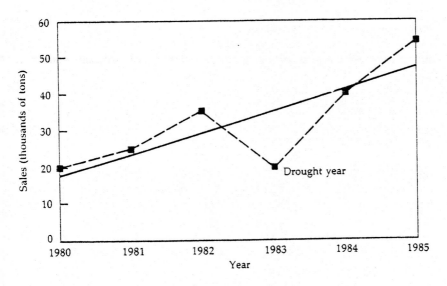

Figure 8. Geographic Distribution of Credit Issued in 1985

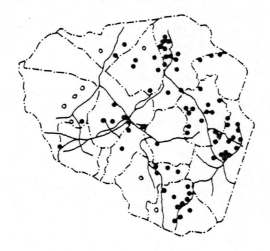

Key: • 10,000 francs of credit issued in a locality; placement of dots is approximate
         and serves merely to show areas of concentration
      ○ 5,000 francs

We have discussed above various modes of communicating monitoring information. The ideal is a suitable blend of all of them. The monitoring staff can prepare written reports, illustrate them with visual displays, and present them in individual or group meetings. Such a course is likely to make a greater impact and to meet the needs of different audiences in the management hierarchy better than a single mode of communication.

Utilization and Management

The utilization of the information generated (assuming it is relevant, timely, and communicated in a readily understood fashion) is a management responsibility. As stated in chapter 1, the existence of an efficient management structure is a prerequisite for an efficient monitoring function. When working well, monitoring enables suitable changes to be made in work plans and activities in the light of new knowledge and experience. A management team that does not possess either the skills or the will to utilize the information provided will not do so, and the information system will atrophy.

There is a distinction between instrumental and conceptual uses of the information. Instrumental use refers to the immediate actions of decisionmakers that result from findings and recommendations. For instance, as a result of monitoring, it is found that some farmers are denied credit through a lack of collateral, and the manager of the credit department takes some action to amend the rules. This is a good example of instrumental use. Conceptual use means that the information influences the thinking of the decisionmakers about a particular issue or intervention strategy even though no immediate action is undertaken or contemplated. In such cases, the information tends to have an educational value. The conceptual uses of the information give justifiable comfort to the monitoring staff; when the data and recommendations are not immediately utilized, it can be hoped that the gradual accumulation of knowledge will influence actions at some time in the future.

7 | Evaluation: Substantive Focus and Types

EVALUATION ENTAILS a systematic, objective analysis of a project's performance, efficiency, and impact in relation to its objectives. Its ultimate purpose is not to pronounce a judicial verdict (although some evaluations do) but to draw lessons from experience in order to adjust the intervention strategy of the existing project, to alter other ongoing projects, or to improve the design of ones to follow. Evaluation is conceived in this book and its companion volume as a way to learn from development efforts so as to improve the development process.

An evaluation attempts to:

- Critically reexamine, in the light of subsequent developments, the project rationale stated in preparation and appraisal documents
- Determine the adequacy of the project to overcome the identified constraints on agriculture and rural development and thus to promote the desired changes
- Compare the actual attainments with the targets set and identify the reasons for shortfalls or overachievements
- Assess the efficiency of project implementation procedures and the quality of managerial performance
- Determine the economic efficiency of the project
- Determine the effects and impact of the project
- Present the lessons learned and the recommendations that follow from them.

This broad agenda will not all be achieved in every case, and some parts of it should only be undertaken selectively. Nevertheless, it gives the scope of the evaluation function. This chapter discusses the substantive focus and types of evaluation undertaken for agriculture and rural development projects. The problems and challenges of assessing project impact are examined in more detail in chapters 8 and 9.

Internal Ongoing Evaluation

Before discussing the formal types of evaluation which are conducted with the involvement of supervisory bodies, governments, or financing agencies, we introduce an important element of evaluation: ongoing evaluation within the project. This is primarily designed for internal consumption and is conducted by the project manager and staff.

Three characteristics of ongoing evaluation need to be mentioned. First, as the name itself suggests, it refers to a continuing process and not to ad hoc exercises. It provides constant feedback to the manager so that corrective actions can be undertaken. Second, it consists of simple, internal exercises which do not involve much data collection. Ongoing evaluations are invariably based on the outputs of the management information system, including the beneficiary contact monitoring and diagnostic studies discussed in earlier chapters. Third, it mainly accents practical recommendations that emerge from the project.

Ongoing evaluation focuses on four sets of questions:

- What is the response of the project beneficiaries to the inputs, services, or other forms of assistance provided by the project? Are the farmers accepting them to the extent anticipated?
- What are the effects of the project on agricultural production? (During the early phases of an intervention, managers are likely to have limited, often impressionistic information on this subject; as the project advances, however, more accurate and reliable information can be gathered, as is suggested in the next chapter.)
- Is the project having consequences which were not intended or anticipated in its design?
- Does the intervention model on which the project is based remain valid in a changing environment?

We have conceptualized the monitoring function, so that most of the areas covered by an ongoing internal evaluation are included in it. In fact, the line dividing the two is very thin; it is not possible to say where monitoring stops and ongoing evaluation begins. Any difference between these two concepts is merely one of emphasis. Monitoring tends to focus more on implementation issues, whereas ongoing evaluation addresses the likely outcomes of the interventions.

The advantages of conducting an ongoing evaluation are obvious. First, it provides systematic feedback to project managers and thus facilitates the integration of the evaluation process into the management system itself. Second, as the ongoing evaluation is conducted by the project staff itself for internal consideration, the staff has a strong motive to assess objectively the project's weaknesses and strengths; they need not be defensive or evasive about its progress. Third, since the staff has intimate knowledge of project activities, the recommendations that emerge from the evaluation process should be practical and relevant. Managers are more likely to implement them than the recommendations of outsiders, who they may believe do not understand their problems or appreciate their perspectives. An ongoing evaluation is not, however, a substitute for external evaluations conducted at the various stages of an intervention. The horizon of managers is undoubtedly limited by their organizational interests and positions, which can prevent them from considering innovative approaches or from questioning the thrust of the implementation strategy.

Focuses of Formal Evaluation

The evaluation process focuses on three areas: performance; output, effects, and impact; and economic and financial efficiency.

Performance

Probably the best understood and least controversial element of an evaluation is the assessment of performance, which broadly defined includes a review of all the activities undertaken by the project to achieve its stated objectives. These could range from constructing physical infrastructure through providing technical advice to the farmers to facilitating the marketing of the outputs achieved. A performance evaluation requires a comprehensive, retrospective look at the project from its inception to the time of the evaluation. The items usually covered in such an evaluation include the following.

- *Project identification, preparation, and appraisal.* The review should include an assessment of the quality of the feasibility studies undertaken, the commitment and capability of the sponsoring agencies, the adequacy of the preparation and appraisal reports, and the time and resources spent on them.
- *Project specification.* The objectives, components, activities, targets, and underlying intervention models should be reviewed with the benefit of hindsight. Some specific questions that an evaluation seeks to answer are: How were the project's objectives determined? Were they consistent with national goals? Were the project components and strategies adequate to achieve the targets? Were the targets realistic? Was the intervention model basically sound?
- *Timing of project start-up and implementation.* The usual questions for evaluation are: Was there an unusual delay in the start-up? If so, what were the reasons and the possible repercussions for the project? Was the project able to complete various activities within the stipulated times?

- *Services and inputs provided.* The adequacy of the supply of the services and inputs to be provided by the project is one key to the assessment of project performance. The supplies are measured against the preestablished targets. The main inputs of agricultural and rural development projects fall into the following categories: physical infrastructure—quantity and quality of construction and whether it was completed when needed; the required timings of utilization; agricultural inputs—volume, quality, and timely supply of inputs, such as credit, fertilizers, seeds, or pesticides; services—agricultural and rural services provided (such as the coverage and quality of agricultural extension) institution building—the extent to which public and private institutions were developed or strengthened.
- *Beneficiary coverage and response.* Some relevant questions are: Did the inputs and services provided reach the target population in the expected numbers? What proportion of the target population was actually covered by the project? To what extent did the target groups use the inputs provided? Were any formal or informal mechanisms for participation established?
- *Managerial performance.* The overall performance of the managers is assessed. Were they able to supervise project activities effectively? Did they establish necessary linkages with governmental agencies and private organizations? Were they task-oriented? Were the human and material resources properly utilized?
- *Financial performance.* Financial outlays are compared with the original cost tables and budgets to examine whether the financial targets and covenants in project agreements were fulfilled and whether in general there has been satisfactory financial control. How were cost overruns financed and underruns redeployed?

Most of the information required for the evaluation of project performance is available within project documents, financial and administrative records, and secondary data available from the executing institutions and agencies. These may need to be supplemented by interviews with principal project staff and representatives of institutions. If the management information system has been set up and the monitoring function carried out in the manner suggested in earlier chapters, the required data will be readily available.

Output, Effects, and Impact

The second focus for evaluation is on the output, effects, and impact of the project. Clearly, a review of performance alone fails to provide a firm basis for such an assessment. It is quite possible for all the activities and tasks expected of a project to be completed satisfactorily within the stipulated time and resources and yet not lead to the anticipated results. For example, service centers have been constructed, and the feeder roads linking farmers to these centers, but they remained unused. Or participatory organizations have been established, but they fell under the control of traditional elites opposed to the very idea of people's participation. Or extension workers have successfully taught the techniques for cultivating a high-yielding variety of maize, but farmers declined to grow it. In each of these instances, an evaluation confined to project implementation based on the original intervention model, would conclude that the project succeeded, although this is hardly the case. In development projects, as in other arenas of human endeavor, well-planned, sincerely executed efforts do not necessarily produce the desired results.

When they are implemented, agriculture and rural development projects generate multiple chain reactions that cannot always be anticipated. Some farmers may benefit, but others may be displaced by economic forces unleashed by the accrual of the initial benefits of these chain reactions. For example, successful promotion of a cash crop may have negative consequences on child nutritional status if the cultivation of food crops for home consumption is affected. Unanticipated consequences are not always harmful; as shown in example 21, a potable water project contributed to increased production and incomes although this was not the objective of the intervention.

EXAMPLE 21. Unanticipated Benefits of a Potable Water Project

A water project provided safe drinking water and improved sanitation to more than 600 villages in Thailand. When evaluated, it was found to have brought about noticeable changes which were positively received in the communities. These changes, however, had little to do with the health-related effects intended by project planners; in fact, communities did not perceive the improved water quality to be of great significance. Instead, villagers were most impressed by the project's impact on water availability—a new network of piped water systems which provided them with reliable and convenient sources of water. This resulted in a considerable saving of time, which in turn allowed them to increase their incomes.

For example, one woman explained in an interview that she used to make at least three thirty-minute trips daily to haul water from a shallow well. Now, however, she paid a nominal service charge for water delivery to her home. With the time the service saved her, she wove mats which she sold in the market to cover the charge. When questioned about the beneficial impacts of the improved water systems, the villagers gave the responses shown in table 4.

The water also helped villagers stabilize food production. In several communities, respondents referred to piped water as insurance against the loss of income during a drought. Before the project, crop failures in these nonir-

Table 4. Benefits Attributed by Villagers to Piped Water Systems

	Number of times mentioned as first, second, or third answer		
Effect	*First*	*Second*	*Third*
More gardening and farming	21	3	—
More craft activities	4	2	—
Increased convenience	4	1	1
Better health	3	—	—
Increased income	3	6	3
More animal raising	2	6	3
More outside jobs	1	1	1

— Nil.

rigated areas forced many men to migrate for employment. According to the villagers interviewed, the water permitted limited irrigation of such high-value crops as garlic and onions and allowed for increased livestock. This cushion diminished the need for seasonal migration.

As evaluated, the project may not have achieved its primary intended purpose of improving rural health. But its unanticipated benefits were assessed as significant by the rural population.

Source: USAID.

Obviously, all the consequences of a project are not visible within a few years. Many, particularly those involving changes in consumption patterns, nutrition, health, and social and economic inequalities may take a long time to develop sufficiently to allow a realistic assessment. Two essential questions are raised concerning the consequences of a project:

- Have anticipated and unanticipated changes occurred, or are they likely to occur?
- Can these changes be attributed to the project's activities?

To answer the first question, we require some indication of the preproject conditions which presumably have been changed, modified, or eliminated. For example, we need to answer such questions as: What were the average yields of maize before and after the project? What were the living conditions of the farmers before and after the project? What was the incidence of malaria in the past and what is it now? We require baseline information to establish benchmarks with which the changes can be compared. And, as we shall discuss in chapter 8, these are not easy to establish.

Addressing the second question poses still more problems. Changes in agriculture or rural society have a multiplicity of causes. Some are directly related to project activities; others have little to do with them. Ideally, to assess the impact of project interventions we need to isolate the project from the impact of exogenous factors either by using experimental and quasi-experimental designs or by relying on such powerful statistical techniques as multivariate regression. In practice, we are rarely able to use such designs or complex statistical techniques because there are no data that meet the rigorous standards these techniques demand. We discuss these issues in detail in the next two chapters. Suffice it to mention here that evaluators in most instances have no option but to draw conclusions on the basis of less rigorous quantitative data supplemented by qualitative information.

Economic and Financial Efficiency

Finally, evaluation aims to determine the efficiency of the project by computing financial and economic rates of return on the money invested in it. Such returns are estimated at the time of project preparation and appraisal on the basis of output models. The purpose of recomputation is to determine, first, whether the original estimates proved to be realistic and, second, the reasons for and implications of any significant variations. Although this subject is of major importance, we can only briefly and generally touch on it, primarily because different agencies follow their own guidelines for computing rates of return.[1]

The difference between financial and economic analysis can be noted briefly. Financial analysis is undertaken from the perspectives of the major participants in the project—various categories of farmers, private firms, governmental agencies, and even the national treasury. It determines in monetary values the costs and benefits to the participants and the net returns derived or expected from their investments. Economic analysis adopts the viewpoint of society as a whole: what did it gain or lose from investing in this particular project?

This simple difference is responsible for three variations in the methods of computation. First, taxes and subsidies are treated as costs and benefits in financial analyses. After all, the taxes paid by the farmer or a firm add to the cost, just as the subsidies received add to the profits. When the project is viewed from the point of view of society, however, taxes and subsidies are simply transfer payments; they are therefore not computed as costs and benefits in economic analyses. Second, financial analyses use market prices of the factors of production whereas economic analyses use shadow prices, which more adequately represent the social costs of capital, goods, or labor. Third, the interest paid to outside

1. See, for example, J. Price Gittinger, *The Economic Analysis of Agricultural Projects*, 2d ed. (Baltimore, Md.: Johns Hopkins University Press, 1982).

individuals or agencies is deducted as a cost in financial analyses. There obviously is no justification for following this course in economic analyses, in which the interest is a part of the total return to the society. (Both financial and economic analyses use discounted cash flow measures.)

There are, of course, several methods of undertaking economic efficiency analysis; two are the effects method and the price-reference method. These are described in detail in various investment agency manuals and texts and are relatively standardized for agriculture and rural development projects. Reservations about their value stem not so much from methodology as from questions about the quality of the data used. If the data are not reliable and adequate, the practical value of such exercises remains limited.

To repeat, every evaluation does not cover the full range outlined in these pages. Significant variations in the coverage of an evaluation depend on the nature, objectives, and components of the project. Moreover, different users of the evaluation findings have different concerns. The supervisory agency may be interested mostly in the performance of managers, the government may be concerned mostly with direct outputs and effects, and international agencies oriented toward alleviating rural poverty may focus mostly on the overall impact in terms of their objective. In addition, practical considerations, such as the available resources, the evaluation expertise of the agency undertaking the evaluation, and time constraints also determine the range of an evaluation.

The Project Cycle and Types of Evaluations

In addition to continuous internal evaluation by project staff, more formal evaluation of an agricultural intervention can be undertaken at many points. The common practice, however, is to carry out evaluations at one or more of three stages of a project:

- In the middle of implementation, when the project has overcome its teething problems, the flow of its services and inputs to the target population has commenced, and its initial responses can be observed
- At the end of implementation, when the project's external funding is over
- Several years after the project's termination, when its long-term effects and impact are visible.

These are known as midterm, terminal, and ex post evaluations. The distinction between midterm and terminal evaluations is not always clear when projects are funded in successive phases. In such cases, an evaluation can be construed as midterm or terminal depending on its recommendations. If the recommendation is to undertake a major redesign that will lead to a radically different second phase, the evaluation might be regarded as the terminal one of the first phase. But the distinction and nomenclature often are only semantic.

Midterm Evaluation

A midterm evaluation typically is carried out three or four years after implementation has commenced. It is the first comprehensive look at the project by the host government and the international funding agencies. What distinguishes it from later evaluations is that corrections to the current project still can be made on the basis of its findings and recommendations. The primary focus of a midterm evaluation is on project performance. Items covered include

- Organizational structure and management capabilities, progress and problems in staff recruitment and placement, ability to get such necessary resources as office space and transportation for project staff, and establishment of organizational linkages with various governmental agencies and organizations
- Procurement of the necessary goods and services from national and international sources (in many projects, procurement delays become a major obstacle to effective implementation)
- Progress in establishing delivery systems for supplying the necessary inputs and services to the target population
- Progress in building physical infrastructure
- Volume and quality of inputs and services
- Initial response by the target population to the inputs and services
- Preliminary indications about emerging outputs
- Changes in the environment since appraisal which are likely to affect performance during the remainder of implementation.

Obviously, at this stage evaluators will not be able to assess the effects and impact of the project. At best, they can critically examine the continuing validity of the assumptions on which the projections of likely impact were based and if necessary amend these in the light of developing circumstances.

Modestly conceived and well-considered midterm evaluations can lead to suitable modifications in project design or strategies, and they can be instrumental in

- Changing the nature of the inputs and services (for example, if there is no effective demand for medium- and long-term loans, the project is asked to confine itself to seasonal loans)
- Modifying the intervention model (for example, if the major impediment to the adoption of innovations is not the nonavailability of

agricultural inputs, as was assumed in the project, but the poor quality of the extension services)

• Shifting the emphasis among target groups (for example, if a large proportion of farmers are women, more attention should be given to their special needs).

Readers of the earlier chapters will recognize the overlap with the monitoring function. If managers demand and obtain an efficient management information system and if it is used to monitor project activities, it will provide nearly all that is needed for this first evaluation exercise by higher authorities.

Terminal Evaluation

A terminal evaluation (also known as a project completion report) is conducted when the funding for the project comes to an end, although of course that does not mean that the services and inputs being supplied by the project cease. In most cases it is assumed that the services will be institutionalized within the system.

The scope of a terminal evaluation is broader than that of a midterm evaluation because, first, the longer time available for review should make possible a reasonable assessment of the initial outputs and effects and, second, the completion of funding requires a careful examination of performance in which all responsible parties give an accounting.

Further, in most cases, the forecast of the impact of the project most likely can be improved on the basis of the evidence accumulated during it. Linked with the estimation of impact are two items which are explored in terminal evaluations: the sustainability of the benefits accruing to the target population and the rates of return on investments.

A terminal evaluation needs to examine the sustainability of the benefits stream because once external funding ends many services and inputs are either discontinued or drastically reduced in quality or quantity. Relevant questions for a terminal evaluation include: What are the realistic prospects of sustaining the benefits stream in the long term? What would be the consequences for project impact if this does not happen? And what can be done about it? It is not always possible, however, to get a very accurate picture of the project's sustainability at this stage.

The rates of financial and economic returns calculated at the time of terminal evaluation should of course be more realistic and accurate than earlier estimates, because at least some of the data required for the calculation are now known with reasonable accuracy. The data on actual production increases and economic gains, however, are likely to be in doubt. As was already indicated (and is discussed further in chapter 8), the terminal evaluation may come too soon for confident estimation of the trends in these variables. To glean the most from the evidence available, the terminal evaluation should review a wide range of data and information gathered from various sources. In addition to the project records, documents, and outputs of the management information system, a search should be made for secondary data that are relevant for a comparison. If necessary, the terminal evaluation should include studies of the beneficiaries' perceptions of the project's benefits and of the impact on their lives.

The recommendations of a terminal evaluation, unlike those of a midterm evaluation, are primarily meant to improve the planning and design of future projects. In some cases, the future project may be a second phase of the one under evaluation, in which case the lessons learned have a direct relevance. But many lessons are generalizable to other similar projects.

Ex Post Evaluation

Often called "impact evaluations," ex post evaluations are designed as in-depth studies of the impact of an intervention and usually are done five to ten years after the completion of its funded implementation. There are two reasons for conducting ex post evaluations. First, as stated above, much of the lasting impact will not be visible at the time the project comes to an end. Second, such impact as is detected at the time of the terminal evaluation might prove transitory. Not uncommonly, agriculture and rural development projects that showed promising gains in early years failed to sustain them in the long run. Conversely, in some instances an outstanding positive impact was produced by a project which was classified as "unsatisfactory" at the time of the terminal evaluation. Example 22 illustrates this with the case of an irrigation and land settlement project which had a lasting socioeconomic impact better than that anticipated at its completion.

EXAMPLE 22. *Better than Anticipated Impact*

The main achievements of an irrigation and land settlement project in Latin America were visible only years after its completion. An ex post evaluation report prepared six years after completion observed that, in spite of difficulties experienced during implementation, the project did indeed achieve its basic goal of stable settlement in the years following completion.

The most striking outcome in the years between its completion and the review was that farmers established strong and efficient organizations. This may have been mostly the result of their surprising response to problems they had encountered during the execution of the project. Less than ideal conditions may have worked in the project's favor: The close cooperation of farmers necessitated by the remoteness of the project area and the strong pioneer spirit of the settlers and government officials helped overcome many of the difficulties associated with new settlements.

Another unanticipated response was a shift in the type of crops grown in the project area. Decreases in the amount of cultivated land and drops in cropping intensity occurred in some areas of the project because of technical design problems. Farmers responded to this potentially serious situation by shifting to higher-value crops, including fruit and rice. This change in turn led settlers and private enterprises to establish fruit-processing facilities and other agroindustries which became highly successful.

Despite errors in the original project design and other setbacks, lasting progress was made. According to the ex post evaluation report, in the years after completion the farmers progressively and successfully took over project responsibilities and even began to function administratively as substitutes for government institutions.

Source: World Bank.

There are several reasons for such developments. Undoubtedly, the most important is that, as a result of the project, long-term changes have been initiated which remove or mitigate constraints on agricultural development. For example, as the evidence accumulates, the government reviews its pricing policies to ensure that farmers have the incentive to avail themselves continuously of the inputs initiated by the project. In other instances, the initial benefits lead to social and environmental changes that further the advances of or inhibit the benefits to the original targeted group. And of course such national forces as a change of government or a large policy shift may eliminate an otherwise substantial project impact or produce an apparent impact that is not in fact related to the project.

Because an ex post evaluation focuses on impact and not on project performance, it must examine these main topics:

- *Farming systems.* The project may cause fundamental changes in cropping patterns, cropping intensities, and cultivation methods. Analogous measures must be determined for livestock, forestry, and fishery projects or components of projects.
- *Employment and work load.* Changes in cropping systems, the introduction of new crops, and the use of new methods and implements tend to have profound effects on employment and work loads for the entire population within the project area.
- *Income.* The measurement of income is important, for productivity increases do not always translate into enhanced incomes for farm families. Lower market prices for crops, more expensive farm inputs, higher taxes, or similar factors can nullify the positive impact on in-

come. However, farmers' incomes are extremely difficult to measure. Farm budgets may be more feasible to evaluate, though this ignores the important role of income from off-farm employment.

- *Living standard.* In addition to or as a substitute for measuring the impact of the project on income, its impact on the general standard of living of the population can be evaluated with such proxy indicators as health and nutrition.

- *Economic inequalities.* Farm households have varying economic and social endowments at the start of the project, and this affects their ability to take advantage of the opportunities for economic advancement that open up. One possible result is that the economic differentiation of the rural society might be accentuated, even in a project with substantial benefits.

- *Gender-based stratification.* Because of their economic, social, and cultural disadvantages, women farmers tend to have little access to the inputs and services provided by the project. Moreover, in those rural societies with a rigid, gender-based agricultural division of labor, innovations in agriculture can affect male and female farmers differently. Therefore, agriculture and rural development impact evaluations focus increasingly on the impact of projects on the conditions of women.

- *Institution building.* The continuing effectiveness of the local development institutions supported by the project must be assessed.

- *Environment.* The positive and negative effects of the project on the natural environment, for example, on soils, water, grazing lands, forests, and wildlife, must be determined.

Example 23 summarizes the major impacts that were observed in an agribusiness project.

EXAMPLE 23. *Socioeconomic Impact of an Agribusiness Project*

A pilot project involved the start-up of an agribusiness company to purchase and freeze nontraditional vegetables for export. The company purchased 11 million pounds of cauliflower, broccoli, brussels sprouts, and similar produce in one year from 2,000 farmers, 95 percent of whom were smallholders. Cultivation in the project area quickly shifted away from traditional food crops to export crops.

An impact study of the potentially wide-ranging consequences of the project included field observation, qualitative interviews, and social surveys. The study found that one reason for the rapid shift to nontraditional crops was that the company established a successful credit program for farm inputs. This opportunity, which had not existed previously in the villages, had increased average investment in small equipment by 200–400 percent. In addition to the direct production impact of the project, significant changes oc-curred in living conditions and in family roles.

The project improved the living standard of much of the local population. Children began attending school instead of seeking paid employment. Poorer families used their higher incomes to better meet their basic needs for food, clothing, and housing. Others used the project-generated income for larger undertakings such as starting stores, purchasing land, building "formal houses," and buying vehicles. Families at all income levels improved and var-ied their diets by expanding their food purchases and eating surplus vegetables not suitable for processing. This marked a significant change from the preproject environment, in which families growing produce for local mar-kets had not been able to afford to consume their own vegetables.

The organization of the traditional family also changed considerably. Women, for example, spent fewer days vending in markets or on household du-ties. More lucrative opportunities for them now existed in agricultural work. Men sought less employment outside the family farm and instead concentrat-ed on meeting the stable demand of the company for produce.

Both the guaranteed demand for their produce and new credit opportunities gave farmers confidence that the key to economic advancement and indepen-dence was expanded commercial production.

Source: USAID.

Ex post evaluations invariably tax the ingenuity of the evaluators, who have to marshal all kinds of evidence to arrive at credible conclusions. Ideally, if the decision to do an ex post study was made at the outset of the project, there will be a time series of relevant data that commences with a baseline at the inception of the project, continues with surveys conduct-ed during implementation and is maintained after completion. Such data generally do not exist, however, so evaluation must make use of such available sources as

- Community statistics which might be collected by the government; China and Bangladesh, for example, collect these regularly
- In-depth interviews with project beneficiaries, government officials, and experts familiar with the area, which are conducted at the time of the evaluation and attempt to trace the history of the changes that have occurred
- A farm survey that attempts to obtain objective data and is commis-sioned specifically for the ex post evaluation
- Project progress reports, midterm and terminal evaluations, and the findings of the diagnostic studies
- Other sources, such as articles, reports, and university theses related to the project or the project area. In one impact evaluation of a rural development project, photographs of the village homes, which had

been taken when the project was initiated twenty years earlier, were used to assess the changes in the living conditions of the target population.

Some form of impact evaluation proposal is included in many of the agriculture projects approved by international funding agencies. The methodology of most such proposals requires annual surveys of randomized samples of beneficiaries. But surprisingly, and naively, most of these surveys are described in appraisal documents as providing the data for an impact analysis by the time that implementation is completed, which is usually five to six years after start-up. The histories of these attempts demonstrate that the planned surveys were not completed in time and even when completed did not produce the type of data needed for impact evaluation.

A comprehensive impact evaluation should be an option used selectively in innovative projects or in those with identifiable and substantial risks. The evaluation staff of a project that requires such evaluation should start collecting data early—preferably at appraisal—and continue collecting them well past completion.

Indicators for Evaluation

The selection of the indicators that will be used to judge project achievements is critical for the conduct of an evaluation. If appropriate indicators are chosen, they help evaluation by

- Revealing the nature and rate of change that has occurred or appears to be occurring
- Enabling progress to be compared with the planned targets
- Assisting in input-output and cost-benefit analyses.

The care needed in selecting indicators for monitoring and the requirements for good indicators were explained in chapter 4. There is no need to recapitulate that discussion because the criteria for monitoring indicators also apply to evaluation. However, four additional observations about indicators for evaluation are appropriate.

First, indicators have a limited contextual relevance and do not possess universal validity. A valid indicator for the living standard of the North-western Province of Zambia is not necessarily a valid one for that of Bangladesh. Infant mortality was a useful indicator for health and nutrition in Western Europe when the incidence of communicable diseases was high and life expectancy was low, but now it has no discriminating value there. It remains, however, a valuable indicator for all developing countries. But, as in this example, some indicators are slow to change and therefore have limited value for normal project evaluation.

Second, appropriate indicators for evaluating a project should be determined at the design or early implementation stage so that arrangements can be made to collect the necessary data. The main criterion for these indicators is that they be sensitive to project-induced change and be measurable without the need for continuous, complex observations of large samples. Just because an indicator such as income seems singularly appropriate does not necessarily mean it can easily be measured.

Third, the number of indicators should be kept to a bare minimum. The temptation to have a large inventory of indicators for multivariate statistical analysis or for safety in case some do not reveal changes should be resisted. Most of the indicators used for monitoring can also be employed for evaluation, but they must be analyzed over a longer time.

Fourth, evaluations should not and cannot always depend on quantitative indicators. Quantitative indicators cannot be constructed for a number of vital consequences. Moreover, the purpose of evaluation is to generate in-depth understanding and not mechanically to report progress or the lack of it. Qualitative indicators should be used to evaluate social consequences in particular. Indicators of people's participation or the changing role of women require such sociological studies and reporting techniques as key informants, unstructured interviews, and participant observation.

Example 24 presents the considerations for the selection of indicators included in the U.N. ACC Task Force on Rural Development publication *Guiding Principles*. Its style may differ from that of the discussion above, but its message is fundamentally the same.

EXAMPLE 24. U.N. Considerations for the Choice of Indicators

An important factor affecting the cost of data collection and the method of analyzing it is the level of the data collected. Indicators may be aggregate at national level, derived from national sources and only applicable at this level. Examples are the gross national product (GNP) derived from national accounts or per capita consumption of calories and nutrients derived from national food balance sheets. A second category of aggregate indicators is derived at the local level (community, village, district). Examples are whether medical services or schools are available in each village/district surveyed and their condition. A third category of indicators is derived from households or individuals, usually through census or sample survey. The degree of literacy and height and weight of children are examples. By and large, aggregate indicators are simpler to collect than household indicators, but because they cannot readily be disaggregated and therefore no distribution data can be obtained from them, they have limited utility. Hence, we cannot use the GNP to arrive at the gross product for a district or for the poor (though regional esti-

mates are sometimes calculated). On the other hand, household data can be disaggregated, but it is generally costly to collect.

Not all concepts lend themselves to relatively simple, quantitative construction of indicators. Examples are the degree of population participation or organizational structure. Rather than trying to squeeze these complex concepts into a small set of numbers, descriptive statements might be prepared with indications of the direction of change.

Implicit in the points above, the number of indicators must be limited to keep information requirements and costs of collection to a minimum and to ensure focus on the most significant issue.

Both indicators and related information requirements should be periodically reviewed to take into account changing needs or refinements in data quality. In this connection, present indicators, or indicators used in other projects, should be reviewed before new ones are considered.

Finally, as far as possible the indicators, or at least some of them, should be divisible by gender, income group, etc., in line with objectives. Disadvantaged groups such as the rural poor and women cannot receive equitable benefits from development projects unless they are specified as beneficiaries, with strategies indicated whereby their disadvantaged position can be overcome and their conditions monitored. To repeat, aggregate indicators cannot usually be divided into sub-categories. Indicators based on the household or the individual are required to provide data separately for men and women or for socio-economic categories such as the poor and the landless.

Source: U.N. ACC Task Force on Rural Development, *Guiding Principles for the Design and Use of Monitoring and Evaluation in Rural Development Projects and Programmes* (Rome, 1984).

Indicators of the quality of life are true proxies for somewhat intangible concepts. Some common proxies either require very large data sets or are so slow to change that they usually are inapplicable. Mortality rates are a striking example of both these limitations. Child nutritional status, school enrollment, expenditure on shelter improvements, and morbidity rates are among the most feasible measures of the quality of life. (Some of these qualitative indicators are described further in chapter 9.)

Beneficiary Assessment of the Project

Systematic efforts should be made to incorporate beneficiaries' assessments of the project into evaluations. Such attempts will undoubtedly enrich the quality of evaluations and will enable the evaluators to draw conclusions that are more relevant, if not necessarily more reliable statistically.

The opinions of beneficiaries, although generally sought in evaluating agriculture and rural development projects, usually remain peripheral.

They often are not even included in the main body of the report. Reservations about their usefulness stem from the premise that farmers' opinions, perceptions, or judgments are highly subjective and thus cannot be valid indicators of the achievement and failures of an intervention. It is often assumed that illiterate, tradition-bound farmers are not able to comprehend the dynamics of the change introduced by a project, much less assess it. Such reservations are totally unsupported by development experience. Three points, however, can be made about what experience does show.

First, there is overwhelming evidence that small farmers tend to assess reasonably accurately the positive and negative outcomes and effects of an intervention. In many instances, their knowledge and judgments actually are more accurate than those of the project staff and other officials who do not know the local conditions intimately.

Second, beneficiaries' should be asked only to assess those aspects of a project of which they are aware, such as the efficiency of input delivery systems, the results of using recommended inputs on agriculture production, and the impact of the project on their living conditions. Certainly they cannot be expected to evaluate organizational structures, procurement systems, and interorganizational relationships.

Third, beneficiary assessment is a supplement to, not a substitute for, the conclusions drawn from objective data. However, the opinions and judgments of the beneficiaries deserve as much weight as if not more weight than those of project staff or government officials.

Chapters 4 and 5 suggested that monitoring staff should study beneficiaries' responses to project services and inputs and conduct diagnostic studies to understand their problems and concerns. Such studies are a good base for beneficiaries' assessments. Of course, additional information will have to be collected at the time of evaluation.

8 | Measurement of Production Increases: Methods and Limitations

ALL THOSE CONCERNED with an agricultural and rural development project—project managers, national authorities, and financing agencies—usually want to evaluate it in terms of how it has increased production. This kind of evaluation aims not only to measure a production gain but also to assess the role of the project in bringing it about. These objectives are likely to be quantified in terms of area and yield increases for specified crops or increased production of livestock and related products. Evaluators may want to go beyond production variables and measure resulting income increases, but it is generally accepted that, within the context of project evaluation, this may be too difficult. At a minimum, it is argued, let the project be evaluated on the basis of production gains. Unfortunately, the evaluators are faced with both theoretical and practical constraints in meeting even this seemingly reasonable demand. Meeting this demand is so commonly attempted in agriculture projects and so rarely achieved that it merits separate treatment. This chapter discusses the scientific framework for establishing change and the causality of change and explains the difficulties in applying this framework in the context of crop production objectives. The chapter emphasizes the difficulty of achieving rigor in such an analysis, and it offers recommendations for a practical form of evaluation linked to production changes. These recommendations require an advance agreement by all parties that the ambitions for and rigor of the analysis will be modest for most projects. In selective cases of innovative or risky projects, a considerable effort may be justified to meet the more demanding standards required by the scientific models.

Two critical steps need to be considered in establishing a framework for an analysis of production benefits:

1. The rate of change of the crop-specific production must be measured either over time or in terms of production by farmers influenced by the project compared with production by those outside its influence.

117

2. A part or all of the rate of change must be attributed to the stimuli offered by the project—to establish causality of change.

Measurement of Change and of the Causality of Change

Example 25 shows the number of observations for different points in time required to fit a trend with sufficient confidence to base an evaluation on it.

EXAMPLE 25. *Annual Growth Rates*

Agricultural projects at appraisal generally illustrate project impact by calculating annual production increases and production targets. Most of the appraisal documents for selected projects involving cereal production anticipated annual growth rates in the range of 4–12 percent.

However, national production statistics reveal a great deal of fluctuation around the trend in annual production because of such factors as climatic and environmental conditions, which cause random variations from year to year, and the impact of such policy changes as those affecting relative prices. It should be remembered that these country-level data often reflect the result of a previous process of "smoothing" in order to adjust figures that appear to depart too far from the trend estimate. Yet selected countries' cereal production trends over a ten-year period reveal an average coefficient of variation around the trend of about 15 percent.

Given this level of "noise" in the system and the desire to detect trends of modest size, the number of time points required to determine that the true trend lies within a certain range of the observed value with a selected level of statistical confidence can be calculated. Table 5 gives these numbers for a range of trend values, two range requirements, and three confidence levels. For example, if a trend is estimated at 6 percent a year and a moderate 85 percent level of confidence is required so that the true value lies within 50

Table 5. Analysis of Hypothetical Trend B

Permitted range around estimate within which B must lie (percent of B)	Confidence level that B is within range (percent)	Estimated number of time points required to measure a trend (in percent) of			
		4	6	8	12
50	95	13	10	8	6
	85	11	8	7	5
	66	8	6	5	3
25	95	21	16	13	10
	85	17	13	11	8
	66	13	10	8	6

percent on either side of this estimate, eight time points are required. In general, it is unlikely that the trends can be measured from a baseline followed by two or three further rounds of a survey, which is all that many projects can achieve.

The mathematics of time series analysis leads inexorably to the conclusion that, to satisfy even modest limits of range and confidence when dealing with trends that are typically anticipated in projects, a high-quality data series needs to be maintained annually over a period that is often longer than the life of a project. These statistical requirements, which are imposed by the study of production that is subject to high annual fluctuations independent of the project, cannot be bypassed or ignored. And the resources available make it difficult to collect data on the scale and of the quality required, even within the life of the project.

These are the fundamental reasons for disappointment with the experience to date in evaluating smallholder agriculture projects. In stark language, the determination of yield or production trends in rain-fed smallholder farming areas may be impossible within the implementation periods of most projects.

The word "rain-fed" is included in this warning because irrigation projects are more promising. Since variation in annual rainfall is a major cause of the large random fluctuations in production time series, the ability to control the amount of water available removes this source of variation and much improves the prospects of detecting a temporal trend with a short time series. Nevertheless, even in states in India where irrigated cultivation is the norm, annual fluctuations are as high as 15–20 percent of the trend line.

The difficulty of measuring a temporal trend, as expressed above, exists without the additional problems by errors in the data—errors that result from basing the observations on a sample or from inaccurately recording the production of a given plot. These errors compound the difficulty and further confound the evaluator.

If the measurement of change is difficult, rigorously attributing the causality of the change is almost impossible under real-life conditions, in which experimental methods and replications cannot be achieved. The experimental method developed by the natural sciences cannot usually be reproduced in evaluation studies of agricultural project participants, as a brief description will illustrate.

The experimental model divides the subjects under study into two groups. One of these will be subjected to the interventions that make up the project. The other, normally called the control group, will not be offered the interventions; it will be isolated from exposure to them. The effect variables are measured in the two groups both before and after the interventions. Differences in the changes in the two groups are attributed to the interventions. If there are discrete interventions or interventions that can be applied at different levels (for example, different application rates for fertilizer), in principle there can be a number of different groups that each receive a particular set or level of intervention. Such an extended system will give more powerful results, since relating changes in the levels of effects to changes in the levels of intervention will clarify the causal relationship.

The constraint imposed by this model is clear. For inferences about cause and effect to be made with established degrees of certainty, the two groups should have identical composition before the interventions are applied to one of them. Precise identity is, of course, impossible, but either the individuals in the groups must be matched according to their position on variables that are thought to influence reactions to the interventions or individuals must be randomly allocated to one of the two groups. Matching variables could be age, sex, socioeconomic status, level of education, area of holding cultivated, or size of household. It is a demanding task to obtain and maintain a successful match on one variable; to do so on several variables is even more difficult. With randomization, the two groups are equivalent at an average level, and neither of the groups is likely to react especially favorably to the interventions. Thus, in a fertilizer trial, land is divided into a number of plots, and the different fertilizer treatments are allocated at random to them. (There are of course much more complicated experimental designs than this simple random model, but they are not relevant to the argument here.)

Matching or random assignment of smallholders is impractical in agriculture and rural development projects. Project locations are not chosen at random, and access to project services cannot be denied to farmers to meet the convenience of the evaluator. Worse still from the evaluator's viewpoint, most rural development projects include diffusion of the knowledge and use of services within the community as a desirable strategy. Such diffusion is desirable for project managers but is undesirable "contamination" of the control group for the experimental model evaluator.

Human reactions may upset the experimental conditions in other ways. In medical trials, the control group is given a placebo—a pill or treatment expected to produce no physiological change—to allow for the possibility that results are being caused by the psychological effects of undergoing treatment of any sort rather than by the effects of the innovation under trial. Such control mechanisms are unavailable in farming, yet it is possible that farmers would react to attention by, say, extension workers regardless of the message delivered. The so-called Hawthorne effect refers to productivity increases stimulated by the act of studying the work group, rather than by any actual changes in conditions of work. It is conceivable that a previously neglected group of farmers might respond favorably to almost any project involving them, no matter what its content. Such productivity gains could of course be considered benefits of a project that arise from its organization rather than its content. But formal impact evaluation will have as its major objective a measure of the effectiveness of the specific interventions offered.

In sum, it is not usually possible in agriculture and rural development projects to establish with any precision the rate of production change within a limited time or to set up an equivalent group study that meets the rigorous requirements of the experimental model. It follows that those responsible for financing or managing rural development must set their sights on evaluations that fall within the confines of what is possible and that the professional evaluator has a responsibility to demarcate these confines and to offer the available options. What are the practical alternatives to a full impact evaluation? Some techniques are introduced below. These are not presented as "quick and dirty," cheap alternatives suitable for use by inexperienced monitoring and evaluation units in developing countries. They, or variants of them, are the *only* options in many project contexts, however well financed the evaluation effort and however experienced the professional staff. Measurement of change over a time series much affected by exogenous forces is subject to mathematical, not resource, limitations, and experimental model designs are likely to be as impractical in real farming communities in the developed as in the developing countries. The brief discussion of the quasi-experimental techniques in the next few pages is intended merely to illustrate the problem facing evaluators and not to be a methodological manual. Indeed, these techniques are outside the options open to evaluators in most projects, and therefore we discuss a less rigorous approach in the last part of the chapter.

The Interrupted Time Series Design

Reference has been made earlier in this chapter to the greater prospect of measuring productivity change in an irrigation than in a rain-fed agriculture project. One reason for this is that a controlled, adequate water supply is available at a discrete moment. It is the classic before-and-after situation, with an observed difference that may be both large and more or less immediate in occurrence. The study of the effect of a change in the producer price is an even sharper example of an evaluation that lends itself to the interrupted time series approach. Although other intervening factors may make attribution of causality difficult, the measurement of change is again facilitated by the clear dichotomy between the before values and the after values. And once again the difference may be large enough to be detected despite annual fluctuations in the time series.

As the name implies, the interrupted time series design works best when the data are available in a regular time series, the intervention is a sharp shock at a discrete point in the series, and the intervention is likely to cause a significant shift in absolute levels of the variable under study. In such cases, it may be possible to detect change and obtain a fair estimate of the magnitude of this change with a time series over a limited number of years. Reliance on such a simple design assumes that the impact of the sudden intervention takes effect almost immediately and is much greater than the normal amplitude of the annual variations. The question of causality is resolved with a modus operandi argument: the provision of water from an irrigation project is expected to produce a major shift in yield levels (indeed, it has been observed elsewhere); the water is provided; and a shift about as large as expected is observed; therefore it is deduced that the project has caused the shift. In other words, the causality linkage is based on commonsense deductions from a comparison between an observation of a reaction to the intervention and a priori expectations about the reaction.

Example 26 shows a successful application of the interrupted time series approach. When the effects of the intervention are likely to be modest in size and perhaps intensify only over a longer time, some way to strengthen the design must be incorporated. This can be done by combining this design with the next one discussed below.

EXAMPLE 26. An Interrupted Time Series

One of the largest agricultural development projects undertaken in Malaysia involved the provision of irrigation works and improved inputs to intensify production on more than 102,000 hectares of prime paddy land. Construction work began in 1966 with the first release of irrigation water taking place in the off-season of 1970. By 1974 the scheme was fully operational: farmers were successfully using double-cropping methods to reach a cropping intensity of nearly 1.98, which far exceeded earlier appraisal estimates.

The data collected over this period show the dramatic impact of irrigation on production levels. During a study period between 1967 and 1974, yields were measured using crop-cutting estimates for each production season. These seasonal data were used to create a time series which reveals very clearly the abrupt 1970 increase in production levels, which then continued on an upward trend (see table 6).

Source: Clive Bell, Peter Hazell, and Roger Slade, *Project Evaluation in Regional Perspective: A Study of an Irrigation Project in Northwest Malaysia* (Baltimore, Md.: Johns Hopkins University Press, 1982).

The Nonequivalent Group Design

The concept of the nonequivalent group design retains the idea of control and treatment groups but without randomizing the allocation of individ-

Table 6. Time Series of Production Levels

Year	Annual gross production (metric tons)
1967	282,674
1968	273,192
1969	279,103
1970	413,055
1971	462,973
1972	553,672
1973	610,405

uals to one group or the other. Individuals from these groups are matched according to certain characteristics at the analysis stage, when it is known to which group each individual belongs. Variables that can be used later in an analysis of covariance or for standardization must be identified before data collection is begun. Examples are the size of the farm, its distance from project services, the availability of family labor, and the use of farm inputs that are not themselves part of the project stimuli.

The advantage of linkage with the interrupted time series design is obvious. If a sample of farmers is observed over time, and some are recorded as adopting the preferred interventions and others as not, it is possible to compare the development of these two groups to improve the discriminant power of the time series analysis. It may also be possible to compare those who used inputs efficiently and obtained a significant shift in production with those who used the inputs but did not achieve such satisfaction. Was there a common factor that may have caused such disappointment, for example, shortage of family labor?

The weakness of the design is that it is prey to the problems of the randomized model which were discussed earlier. Causal inferences will be weakened by the inability to demonstrate whether or not causes other than the project interventions were responsible for observed differences between the two groups. Environmental and maturation effects are likely to be aggravated with nonequivalent groups. Living subjects will naturally change over time—mature—and this will complicate the assessment even if the groups are equivalent at the outset. Some environmentally induced changes may be larger than those anticipated from the project. Differential maturing is particularly likely as the adopters of the project interventions probably consist of the more energetic and able or of those who are in some other way in a position to benefit most from the project. Example 27 outlines a study of the impact of extension services in a state in India. The difficulty of establishing causal inferences is well exhibited in the description of the complexity of this analysis.

*EXAMPLE 27. The Rigor of Analysis Required to Measure
the Impact of Extension Services*

*In 1982 the World Bank and Haryana Agricultural University began a study
in northwest India to examine the impact of the training and visit (T&V) system of extension on agricultural production. Two areas were selected that
were agroclimatically and culturally similar. In one area (Karnal district in
Haryana State), a T&V system was introduced in 1979; in the other (Kairana
tehsil [subdistrict] in Uttar Pradesh), the traditional extension system still
operates. A detailed survey of farms was conducted in 1982–83 to analyze productivity differentials between the areas for two crops, a high-yield variety of
wheat and rice.*

*An extensive set of explanatory variables had to be taken into account. The
first step was to use econometric techniques to control for variations in quantities of variable and fixed inputs, soil types, human capital, irrigation (both
quantity and quality), and the production environment. The possibility of systematic differences in microclimatic conditions which would not be measured
by these variables had already been minimized by including in the survey only
farmers in Kairana tehsil that were located less than thirty miles from Karnal
district.*

*Once the influences of these explanatory indicators were known, the second
step was to determine the disembodied productivity differential. The disembodied productivity differential showed the difference in output between
farmers in Karnal and Kairana tehsil when explanatory indicators were controlled for and when the same amounts of physical production inputs were
applied. If initial productivity levels were equal, this differential should have
represented the impact of training and visit extension messages involving better utilization and timing of inputs, the adoption of better practices, and the
timely responses to problems encountered by farmers during the season.*

*Additional differences in agricultural productivity could have been the re-
sult of the greater use of physical production inputs induced by the reformed
extension system and not only of better management. Embodied differentials,
however, cannot be identified from an analysis of the relationship between the
outputs and inputs alone. Their estimation requires an analysis of the supply
of output and the demand for inputs as functions of such exogenous variables
as fixed inputs and the prices of output and inputs. This was not fully feasible
because the price data were not sufficient for such an analysis, and embodied
effects were thus eventually ignored even though some indirect estimates
were obtained.*

*Once the disembodied production differential had been estimated, one
problem still remained. If there were any unaccounted-for fixed and systematic differences between Karnal and Kairana tehsil or if there had been more
rapid diffusion of knowledge in one of the areas before the initiation of T&V extension, then the productivity levels in earlier years would not be equal. The*

third step would be to subtract this initial productivity differential from the estimated productivity differential for 1983. Only then would any remaining productivity differential in favor of Karnal indicate a positive impact of T&V extension.

In the absence of a similar farm survey for 1978–79 (pre-T&V season), data derived from seasonal crop-cutting estimates had to be used to provide a time series of mean yields of wheat and rice. These mean yields, however, include in any given year random elements which fluctuate over time, such as severe pest problems or adverse weather conditions. Hence, a number of detailed adjustments were undertaken to derive a measure of the baseline productivity differential, which was consistent with the evidence derived from the detailed farm sample survey carried out in 1982–83.

Source: Gershon Feder, Laurance Lau, and Roger Slade, *The Impact of Agricultural Extension: A Case Study of the Training and Visit System in Haryana, India.* World Bank Staff Working Paper 756 (Washington, D.C., 1985).

The weaknesses inherent in this design have been duly stressed, but it remains the closest practical design option for formal, scientific impact analysis. Inferences will be based on plausible interpretation of the data rather than statistical rigor, but this is a necessary modification of the ideal in real-life projects.

The Counterfactual Argument

A popular method of presenting the expected benefits of a project at the time of its preparation or appraisal is to model the future course of events without any interventions and then forecast the changes that the interventions will induce. In principle, the latter can then be observed and compared with the former. This method is known as a counterfactual argument. For development projects that are expected to generate only modest increases in productivity, an extreme form of this argument is to postulate that the position of the intended beneficiaries would have *deteriorated* but for the stimuli provided. This may be true, but it is difficult to demonstrate. To be credible, the argument must be derived from a strong data base that predates the project. Unfortunately, smallholder, rain-fed farming projects tend to assume static or "deteriorating" without-project situations, and these projects typically lack a sound data base at the time of preparation.

The main problem of this argument, from the point of view of the evaluator, is that when it is presented in project documentation it assumes that the growth curves for the situations with and without the project are both stable. The presentation of such a regular time series would appear to offer a clear evaluation objective. But, in fact, the actual time series with the project will have the high levels of random fluctuations discussed earlier, and the time series without the project often is based on an assumed level in year zero and a hypothetical trend, neither of which may be realistic. It is not uncommon for an initial survey of yields to produce estimates that differ greatly from those assumed in calculating the expected benefit stream. This might not seem a major difficulty, for this calculation could be rerun. But all parties are reluctant to accept that the assumed base data and simulated time series are wrong. Rather, the evaluator's observed data are immediately regarded as suspect, and the whole evaluation effort is seen as dubious.

The Limits of Ambition for Impact Evaluation

The arguments above clearly show that the rigor of the survey design and long time frame (from before commencement to well past disbursement) will demand so many resource inputs and such a long-term objective to measure a project's lasting impact that it can be undertaken only selectively. The pseudo-experimental designs outlined above may make such studies more feasible, but the difficulties still are considerable.

At this point, it is useful to review the different levels and timings of evaluation objectives. During the implementation of the project, qualitative and simple quantitative information from its beneficiaries (discussed in chapters 4 and 5) provides a first assessment of its effects. At the completion of implementation (about five to eight years from initiation), there is a need for a preliminary assessment of the project's lasting results: production increases and their socioeconomic consequences. Time series analyses will likely require a longer time span, and comparative group studies may have proved impossible to set up because of the diffusion effects of the project. Evaluation probes of selected farmers may provide a plausible subjective assessment of the change attributable to the project. Less ambitious evaluations offer practical opportunities for the use of small-scale studies, depending on the degree to which the results can be generalized. We consider the possible uses of small-scale studies in this context.

The methods described above, implicitly assume that the evaluation objective is to measure impact in terms of the total or average changes for the entire population covered by the project. The data reflecting change, must therefore be derived from probability samples which may need to be at least in the hundreds.

It is necessary to distinguish between two components of the evaluation objective as stated above. First is the *number* in the total population who have benefited from the project (which can be classified according to the categories of adoption and so on discussed in chapter 4). Second is the measurement of the *average change* in the output variables achieved by these beneficiaries, over and above the change experienced by those who have not been exposed to project interventions.

There are only two valid ways to estimate the number of people who have benefited from project services. The number may be obtained by summing the lists of names available in project records. Or if such details are not available, a probability sample must be selected in order to estimate the number within a given margin of error.

Credit projects provide an obvious example of the first option. It would be a strange credit bank that did not maintain records of the names and addresses of its credit recipients. Extension projects (of the classic type) provide an example of the second. Lists of farmers exposed to the message regarding use of inputs will not normally exist. Even if extension agencies keep a list of so-called direct contacts, the message is diffused through local communication and perhaps on the radio and at group meetings. To estimate the number who have received the message therefore requires probability sampling techniques. Note, however, that the number who understood the message and purchased the input may be known from records of sales by the farm service centers or other outlets. Names will not be known, and the list will contain those who may have become users of the input for reasons totally unconnected with the project.

Estimating the proportion of a population that belongs to a certain subgroup requires very carefully selected sampling techniques that meet randomization requirements. No selection based on subjective criteria or other informal methods will do. But the sample required to estimate such a proportion need not be very large (see chapter 4; more details in chapter 6 of the companion volume). Moreover, interviewing to determine if the respondents are receiving project services or are aware of a particular recommendation is not an arduous task. There thus seems little reason why an accurate evaluation of the number of beneficiaries and their agrodemographic profile cannot be made at the completion of a project.

The second component of the evaluation objective, the measurement of differential change within the population, provides some opportunities for the application of case study methods. As will be seen, the interpretation of the case study results requires care because they cannot be scientifically generalized to a wider population. But such methods can aid in doing the pragmatic evaluation required in the report at the completion of implementation.

The term case study is used in various ways in evaluation literature. It often describes a detailed report on one particular case, event, or project. In this and the companion volume, the term refers to the study of a very small number of units in the population, which are selected (usually, in a subjective manner) to represent particular subgroups of the population but which do not necessarily include all identified subgroups. Because of the method of selection, generalizing the results, even for subgroups, is an act of faith, not of science.

Case Studies to Disprove a Hypothesis

One of the most powerful uses of case studies is to disprove a hypothesis that is fundamental for the implementation strategy. Suppose that, in order to benefit from a proferred set of services, a farm household must be prepared to clear and prepare land more thoroughly than it has done. It is assumed that the cost of this will be perceived by the farmer to be small compared with the ensuing benefits. Careful interviews with and observations of a few farm households (chosen because of their different family sizes) reveal that except for large families the incremental labor input either is, or is perceived to be, greater than the family has available or can afford. It is then unnecessary to estimate precisely how many families will not undertake this necessary first step. The case study is sufficient to demonstrate that a fundamental assumption of the project strategy may be wrong; the need for further examination of the strategy is indicated.

Case studies based on nonrandomized selections or on randomized selections of insufficient size cannot be used for valid inferences about the incidence of a phenomenon in the population or the average value of a variable in the population. But they can be used to disprove a null hypothesis that a particular constraint does not exist or a particular activity is open to all members of the population. As Casley and Lury state, "One advantage of the case study method [is that] one may not be able to generalize from it, but one may be able to reject existing generalizations. A number of case studies have certainly been important, for example, in undermining widely held views about the irrationality of peasant economic activities."[1]

This use of a case study is strengthened if it focuses the range of inquiry for a subsequent sample survey by suggesting the indicators to include in it. For example, a case study may reveal that an average farm family has a particular labor constraint at a certain season if they grow both crop A and crop B. They will therefore resist changes that demand a further labor input at that time. A follow-up sample survey can establish the true proportion of farm families whose actions will be based on this constraint.

This use of a case study is particularly appropriate at the appraisal or early implementation stages of a project. To demonstrate a fundamental flaw in the project strategy at the time of evaluation may be necessary but

1. Dennis J. Casley and Denis A. Lury, *Data Collection in Developing Countries* (New York: Oxford University Press, 1981).

is certainly belated. Nevertheless, if there is a disappointing number of acceptors of project interventions, to question basic assumptions at the evaluation stage by using a case study may help to adjust the strategy for the later stages of implementation.

Case Studies for Assessing Production Changes

A first attempt at evaluating the project in terms of productivity increases will be needed for a completion report at the end of the implementation stage. Even if a time series of area and yield data for the geographical region or population covered by the project has been maintained, it may not be of sufficient length.

At the time of appraisal, the expected production increases will have been estimated, probably on the basis of farm models. If a monitoring system as advocated in this volume was established in good time and maintained during the project life, some of the coefficients of several of the parameters in the model will be better known at the time of completion than at appraisal. One method of evaluation is therefore to rerun the model using the monitoring data base. But the model itself can be improved by using actual case studies to revise the expected productivity increases.

The project assumed that, if certain recommendations or inputs were adopted or certain services made available, production benefits would result. The monitoring system should provide estimates of the numbers who adopted in full measure, adopted partially or without proper farming techniques, and those who neither adopted nor participated in any way. The second category may of course be a continuum of a range of partial use of project services.

Reasonably early in the project, it should be possible to identify the full adopters who should be reaping all the expected benefits. A few of them should be selected and their cooperation elicited so that full farm performance data can be maintained. Cooperation is more important in this respect than random selection. What is being tested with this case study is the ability of the project package to deliver the postulated benefits under favorable recipient conditions. In statistical jargon, the cases are intended to represent the upper tail of the responding population.

Similarly, during the project life, some farmers should be identified who, according to their reaction and project staff observation, have tried the recommendations or inputs but are not detecting significant benefits. Diagnostic studies of these should have been launched as part of the management information system described in chapter 5.

The evaluator may therefore have estimates of benefits from the best performers and studies that show whether partial adopters (or adopters in unfavorable circumstances) obtain any significant benefits at all.

Given the numbers in these various categories from the monitoring system, it should be possible to make some inferences regarding the success of the project.

The approach being taken is related to the concept of the quasi-experimental design outlined earlier in the chapter. In the early stages of the project, the population has divided itself into groups that can be identified by interviews carried out by project staff. These groups may be classified as:

- Full adopters with good application of new techniques who are satisfied with the results as they perceive them
- Adopters of selected parts of the recommendation package that require little change to farming practices
- Those who claim to have been adopters but who have rejected the techniques because of their dissatisfaction with the results
- Those who did not adopt although given the opportunity
- Those who had no access to the project services and recommendations.

These groups, of course, are changing; evolving, it may be hoped, toward a growing number of full adopters. The essential feature is to obtain area and yield data on a few cases in at least the most important of these groups, notably the full adopters and those who have rejected the techniques, while relying on the monitoring function within the project to report on the numbers eventually contained in each group.

High-quality observations and carefully elicited farmers' perceptions of the changes the project has induced are the keys to successful case studies. That is why respondent cooperation is crucial. It may be possible, for example, to persuade a few full adopters who are pleased with their relationship with the project to keep a simple diary of their farm inputs and outputs. The disgruntled may not be so cooperative and may require a more supportive approach to data collection, including objective measurements. In any case, direct observation is desirable to verify that although a farmer is adopting the recommendations in a realistic way he is truly not reaping significant gains.

If the monitoring system allows the sizes of adopter groups to be calculated and individuals to be identified, there is no reason why randomization of selection should not be introduced at the last stage of respondent identification. Many evaluators feel this to be necessary to achieve respectability. But numerical inferences about the population at large is not the purpose here. The goal is to develop a detailed confirmation that for an important group—those who take full advantage of the offered services—the implementation strategy worked and the production benefits are beginning to appear. This confirmation is supplemented where possible by a diagnosis of why the strategy is not working for others, so that lessons may be learned and the design of later projects improved.

It is possible to expand the number of cases in the study and randomize the selection but still get the worst of both worlds for two reasons. First, the sample size is still too small to provide low sampling errors but is too big to provide the high-quality interviews and observations that are possible only when the number of cases is very limited. Second, the focus on satisfied and dissatisfied customers is lost in the random selection process.

The presentation of the results of such an evaluation is critical. Inferences regarding the magnitude of production increases for the population should be avoided. The numbers in the various groupings can be given if the monitoring system was successful. Comments on productivity gains should be couched in such terms as:

> Among the most successful responders to the project, records maintained for _____ of these show that they achieved output gains as follows: _____. This indicates that the technical package was effective for at least these particular cases. Studies of _____, however, revealed that the benefits do not emerge when the following conditions pertain: _____.

To be realistic, one must expect that in completion reports that require a reestimation of the economic rate of return of a project, the economist may make inferences from case study material which in effect imply generalizing to the population at large. The limited value of such a calculation must be recognized, but it will be better than merely rerunning the original model with the ex ante, and probably optimistic, assumptions of area and yield changes.

9 | *Special Topics in Impact Evaluations*

THE EXTENDED DISCUSSION in the previous chapter on the measurement of production increases in agriculture was justified by the frequency with which this is attempted. But other measures are equally important and problematic in evaluating a project's impact on living standards. These measures need to be carefully reviewed for possible inclusion in the evaluation, especially for projects with intervention models that are not well tested or for large-scale interventions which may have an uncertain impact on a widely dispersed population.

The cautions given in the previous chapters about the ambition to establish causal relationships based on quasi-experimental designs and sophisticated statistical analyses pertain even more to the measurement of socioeconomic consequences of a project than to the measurement of agricultural yields or livestock production. Socioeconomic measures are not without ambiguity and experts differ seriously about how to define them and how to use them in an operational context. Although indicators have been constructed for these purposes, their status remains problematic. Target group participation, for example, cannot be measured as precisely as maize yields or dairy production and cannot be expressed in terms that are universally accepted.

This chapter focuses on five areas of potential impact: incomes and standards of living, nutrition, the participation of target groups, the status and role of women, and the environment.

Incomes and Living Standards

The primary objectives of development interventions are to engender sustained economic growth in project areas and to alleviate poverty. Changes in incomes and living standards are the most direct and important measures of project impact.

In most projects, smallholders are the main group targeted to receive the inputs and services that are designed to increase production and productivity. Landless agricultural workers, however, also benefit. Higher

132

productivity often requires more labor-intensive operations, which contribute to increased employment opportunities and higher wages. For example, improved irrigation and hybrid seed enable farmers to increase cropping intensity greatly and thus to harvest larger quantities, thereby expanding their need for labor. Nonagricultural workers also profit from the expanded opportunities created by the project in other sectors, such as transportation, marketing, processing, servicing, and repair. As with other development initiatives, agricultural projects have backward, forward, and lateral linkages with the economy that increase incomes and improve the living conditions of the rural population.

Despite favorable aggregate results, the conditions of some groups may worsen because of a project. In large irrigation projects, for example, some farmers without the security of land titles are likely to be dispossessed. Increased mechanization promoted by a project can deprive landless agricultural workers of their only means of livelihood.

Indicators

The postulated economic benefits of a project are usually expressed in terms of income. As indicated earlier, however, in the case of small farmers it is difficult to define and measure income accurately; in fact it has rarely been done. It may be possible to obtain data on income from a cash crop, particularly one marketed through a limited number of traders or agencies whose records provide a check on farmers' responses. Prices of crops or other agricultural products (collected regularly at selected markets or buying centers) along with estimates of production can be used to calculate independent estimates of cash receipts. In aggregate terms for a zone or stratum, such an estimate of total income may be satisfactory for evaluating the economic benefit of particular crops or products.

If total farm or household incomes need to be measured, the difficulties become extreme. There are definitional problems caused by such factors as the consumption of home production and the valuation of labor inputs. There are also response problems. Income generation is erratic because of sporadic marketing; the income of each household member is difficult to obtain from a single respondent; and informal activities that produce income, such as beer brewing or small-scale trading, are notoriously difficult to cover in an income survey. Moreover, income is always a particularly sensitive topic of inquiry for most respondents; objective responses are not elicited easily.

The measurement of expenditure avoids some of these definitional and response problems. Many budget surveys record expenditure more accurately and completely than income, and many reports which contain cross-tabulations of one variable against income classes use expenditure classes as a proxy for these income groups. Expenditure can be recorded fairly accurately if the recall and reference periods are appropriate. For casual daily expenditures, the recall period may need to be no longer than two to three days. Such items as rent, services, and school fees may need a reference period of one month; and irregular major expenditures on household or farm items may be reported annually. Problems of prestige expenditures made in an attempt to impress have to be considered.

There is not an exact equivalence between expenditure and income, but for many population groups changes in expenditure reflect changes in income fairly accurately. Can expenditure then be used as a proxy for income in evaluating change? The answer to this is only a qualified yes because expenditure surveys may require multiple visits for an extended period in order to assess total expenditure for the period. The almost continuous maintenance of such a survey should not be undertaken lightly. Since major expenditures can be recollected for a fairly extended period, the problem is the frequency of visits required to estimate average daily minor expenditures. One possibility is to conduct a one- to two-week survey (with several visits within the period), repeated at certain selected times in the year (to reflect, say, preharvest, postharvest, and other major seasonal highlights) and to average the daily expenditures recorded in each of these phases of the survey.

Information about expenditures may also require multiple interviews in a household. In many societies, women and men differ in their sources of income and in their expenditures, and neither sex has much information about the expenditures by the other.

The use of expenditure in this way needs to be carefully tested in each situation, but it may well be an easier method and a more accurate indicator of income change than an inaccurate record of actual income.

The quality of housing and related facilities indicates the economic circumstances of a household; we can reasonably assume that an improvement in the economic conditions of a family will be reflected in a better dwelling and improved facilities. Some of the items that can be used to construct an indicator of the quality of housing are:

- Size, such as the covered area or number of rooms
- Type of construction material, such as brick, stone, or wood
- Nature of the roof, such as thatched, tiled, or concrete
- Access to potable water
- Location of bathrooms within the dwelling

The impact of increased incomes may be more visible in internal improvements to a house and in the acquisition of durable possessions than in changes in the building. Possessions may be more sensitive to short-term changes. Items such as bedding; the quality of clothing; footwear; cooking utensils; basic furniture (cots, stools, chairs, and so forth); and such sundries as a watch, radio, or bicycle have been used to construct an indicator of the living standard.

The availability of community facilities is an essential component of the living standard. Moreover, many rural interventions are specifically designed to improve and expand community facilities. Access to primary health facilities (measured either by the existence of a facility or the distance traveled to seek assistance), all-weather roads, and primary schools therefore can be used as an indicator. Community facility indicators can be derived easily from existing records or documents or from simple field observation. Because the data are collected at the village and not household level, the collection process is economical. Example 28 outlines twelve indicators that were used to measure the standard of living in a study in India.

EXAMPLE 28. Measurement of the Living Standard

A study in the Indian state of Kerala used a number of indicators to measure the living standard. Below are some excerpts.

Household income *in cash and kind from all sources. Respondents were requested to state their monthly income from all sources in cash and kind with specific ranges.*

Income per adult equivalent. *"Mid" points were fitted to the above ranges, taking account of the distribution. This figure was then divided for each household separately by the number of persons in the household, counting persons aged 15 or over as one, children under 15 as one-half of a person.*

Type of house. *A fivefold classification was used: 1. roof and wall of leaf; 2. roof of leaf; wall of mud, unburnt brick, or softwood; 3. roof of leaf; wall of stone, brick, or solid timber; 4. tiled roof, any [kind of] wall; 5. concrete structure.*

Furnishings. *A fourfold classification was used: 1. bare essentials; 2. sparse; 3. moderate; 4. sufficient. "Moderate" furnishings would, for example, include a table, a few cots, and a sufficiency of utensils. "Sufficient" would be anything beyond this level.*

Sanitation. *A fourfold classification was used: 1. flush toilets; 2. borehole with water seal; 3. covered pit; 4. other (open air).*

Electricity. *Whether the house is connected to the mains or not.*

Water. *A fivefold classification was used: 1. piped water inside premises; 2. piped water outside premises (shared); 3. protected well inside premises; 4. protected well outside premises (shared); 5. unprotected (pond, river, stream, unprotected well, etc.).*

Footwear. *Whether footwear of any kind is regularly used, with distinction made between households where all persons aged 2 years of age or over regu-*

larly wear shoes; more than half use footwear, fewer than half do so; none do so.

Food consumption. *After considerable experimentation and with some hesitation, the following indicators were used: 1. expenditure on food plus consumption from own produce valued at local retail prices per adult equivalent; and 2. whether there was expenditure during the reference week on one or more of the following "non-essential" items: fruit, vegetables, pulses, cereals other than rice, milk, milk products.*

Primary education. *Households were classified according to whether all person aged 6–19 in the household had either completed primary education or were still at school, or whether one or more persons had left school with incomplete primary education or had received no schooling at all.*

Household possessions. *Nine possible possessions were noted in the schedule: bicycle, motorcycle, car, radio, refrigerator, electric fan, time piece (watch or clock), and sewing machine.*

Land held. *Total land owned or rented by the household, including the site of the house, but excluding land rented out or owned by family members not part of the household.*

A number of possible indicators were rejected, mainly on technical/statistical grounds. For example, while morbidity data are available for households, relatively few cases of morbidity were reported. It cannot be assumed that households not reporting illness in the seven previous days are in general healthier than households with a case of illness reported. The difference may be the chance result of a visit during one, rather than another, week. It may be valid to calculate morbidity rates for the area, but not for the household. Other examples: since virtually all houses in rural Kerala are owner-occupied, information on whether a home is owned or rented has no significance in rural areas; annual expenditure on medical, educational, and other items was found to be unreliable and could not be used.

Source: Wolf Scott and N. T. Matthew, *A Development Monitoring Service at the Local Level* (Geneva: U.N. Institute for Social Development, 1983).

Of course, all the indicators in the example should be constructed with reference to local conditions during a specific period. In many instances, a few indicators of the living standard will serve the purpose, especially if the areas covered by the project possess considerable socioeconomic homogeneity. A short list of particularly relevant indicators remains our strong recommendation.

Data Collection Strategies

There are three principal strategies for assessing the effects of specific interventions. The first is to conduct a baseline household survey of preproject conditions and then to conduct further surveys to measure longitudinal changes in the incomes and living conditions of the target population during and after the project. Depending on the nature of the survey design, the same respondents can be reinterviewed over a period of time or a fresh sample can be constructed for each succeeding survey. The advantages of each of these sample designs are discussed in chapter 5 of the companion volume.

Despite its obvious attractiveness, this strategy is not practical in most cases. Most projects or sponsoring agencies are unable to muster the resources that are needed to conduct the household surveys—a cadre of highly trained technical personnel and an efficient team of enumerators. As demonstrated in chapter 8, annual agricultural yields vary greatly, which affects the earnings of farmers. Therefore, establishing trends in income and the living standard presents the same problem as was noted for measuring production trends: many points in time are required. The data generated by such surveys are also likely to be poorer than the estimates of production for the reasons outlined earlier. It is therefore hardly surprising that one rarely finds an impact evaluation of an agriculture and rural development project that has successfully utilized income data from baseline and follow-up surveys.

The second strategy is to conduct a single, cross-sectional household survey at the end of the project or a few years after its completion. This survey asks objective and subjective questions about the changes in respondents' incomes and living standards. Its objective questions can gather data for a comparison of the incomes and expenditures of project beneficiaries with those of other population groups. Its subjective questions can be such probes as, "What kind of roof did you have ten years ago?" and "What kind of roof do you have now?" In addition, the respondent can be asked to evaluate change. For example, we can ask, "Do you think that your housing conditions have been the same / gotten better / gotten worse during the past ten years?" Questions such as these help capture the changes that have occurred during the intervening years. The data generated by a single survey of this type cannot be as useful as those collected by baseline and follow-up surveys. But a single household survey can provide valuable information at a reasonable cost. An added advantage is that the evaluators can be involved in data collection and analysis.

The third strategy is to seek the views of local experts, government officials, and leaders through in-depth interviews or informal surveys. One limitation of this strategy is that assessments may be biased by organizational interests and ideological commitments. Government officials may paint a positive picture while village leaders insist that little has changed for the better. The evaluators will have to draw their own conclusions after interviewing a cross-section of the key informants.

These three strategies can be combined. Moreover, the data they generate can be supplemented by such suitable secondary data sources as censuses, agricultural surveys, and community statistics. Many countries are attempting to develop a capability to conduct rural household surveys of income, expenditure, and living standards. The World Bank is testing a Living Standards Measurement Study model. Any evaluator embarking on such a survey is advised to consult the national statistical authorities and to refer to the manuals and reports of such pilot studies.

Nutrition

Nutritional status is essentially a component of the living standard, but we discuss it separately because of its paramount relevance to the lives of the rural poor. Changes in the nutritional status of the target population often tell more about the impact of an intervention than any other indicator. One advantage of focusing on nutritional status is that relevant data and information can be gathered with relative ease.

Successful projects contribute to increased agricultural production, which translates into enhanced food consumption as a result either of increased food availability or of the income generated by the marketing of surpluses. Moreover, increases in the incomes of farmers and agricultural workers enable them to buy medicines, and general improvements in economic conditions also result in better hygienic conditions and thus improve health and nutritional status. The cumulative result is that agricultural interventions tend to have positive effects on general nutrition. In certain instances, of course, the nutritional status of some groups may be affected adversely by agricultural projects. An overemphasis on cash crops can contribute to the general neglect of traditional food crops. Income earned from sales of crops may not be spent on food for the family. Land clearance projects have occasionally deprived local tribal groups of the edible wild life that existed on the land before it was cleared for agriculture. Such possibilities affect the analysis of a project's impact.

A few general observations can be offered about the measurement of nutritional status. (As with income, the reader is referred to the technical documentation available from such agencies as the FAO, WHO, and UNICEF if a nutrition survey is contemplated.) Since the nutritional status of target populations has many factors and conditions, it is very difficult to establish a causal relationship between the project and changes in nutrition. In general, it is enough to determine at the completion of the project whether the nutritional status of various groups has improved or worsened and to draw plausible inferences from these findings that do not carry causality too far.

Quantitative data from a set of carefully selected indicators will often need to be supplemented by in-depth qualitative studies—especially when project effects can be both beneficial and harmful. For example, consider a project that has generated considerable employment for rural women. On the one hand, this will increase the income and purchasing power of women workers, who are likely to buy more food and thereby improve the nutrition of their families. On the other hand, their employment may affect child rearing, food processing, cooking time, and vegetable cultivation. Some of these changes might be detrimental to the nutritional status of the children. In such cases, qualitative studies can help us understand complex relationships between specific interventions and nutritional status.

Indicators

It is preferable for two reasons to collect data on nutritional status from children in the target population: first, children up to five years of age are the most vulnerable to malnutrition; second, the effects of changed conditions are more easily visible in them than among adults. The best indicators of nutritional status for the evaluation of rural projects are such anthropometric indexes as those listed below.

- *Weight at birth*. This indicator is based on the incidence of low birth weight in a population and is computed as the proportion of the children born under 2.5 kilograms. Obviously, precise measurements of newborn babies are possible only when they are delivered either in a maternity clinic or under the direct supervision of a trained nurse at home; since these are not common practices in rural areas, the use of this indicator is limited.
- *Weight for age*. Young children (usually between one and five years of age) are weighed, and their precise age is recorded. Weight for age is calculated as the weight of the child as a percentage of the expected weight for that age given by international standards (sometimes calculated using local data sets).
- *Height for age*. This is calculated on the basis of the height of the child with reference to the expected height of a child of that age. A level below 90 percent of the expected height indicates stunting. A more precise measure for young children is the *length* of the child.
- *Weight for height*. This indicator is utilized in conjunction with the height for age. A weight for height ratio below 80 percent of the standard indicates wasting.

The FAO is at present experimenting with these indicators for adult populations; however, no definitive findings are available.

The choice of the child population from which a sample is drawn is of course dependent on the scope of the evaluation. If school attendance is high, a survey of school children six to nine years old might be convenient despite the inherent bias. But in general the measurements should be based on a sample drawn from and measured in the household setting.

In addition to the anthropometric indexes, mention must be made of mortality and morbidity rates.

- *Infant and child mortality rates.* Infant mortality rates are expressed as deaths per thousand live births during the first year of life. Child mortality rates are computed in the same way, except that the age group included is one to five years of age.
- *Morbidity rates.* Morbidity rates can similarly be calculated using some agreed measure of sickness and frequency of occurrence.

These rates are among the most widely used indicators at the national level. For two reasons, however, infant and child mortality rates have limited use in assessing the impact of a development project. First, adequate records about births and deaths are not kept regularly in villages, and therefore the data are not reliable. Second, the size of the population covered by the project must be large in order to draw valid conclusions. Mortality, fortunately, is not a common event, so to estimate the rates requires very large samples.

On the whole, anthropometric indexes best measure nutritional status in rural areas. They are economical and can discern short-term variations in the nutritional status of populations. For example, in a national program on nutritional surveillance, anthropometric data were recorded and analyzed from three clinics; figure 9 gives these data. The ability to detect change is clear from the plotted graphs, which capture variations for even a short time span of eighteen to thirty-six months. A trend toward improvement is visible after analysis of only eighteen months' data for all the clinics, despite monthly variations. Clinic B, for which thirty-six months' data were analyzed, improved particularly markedly. The data also show seasonal variations in nutritional status.

Data Collection Strategies

Three strategies for data collection to measure nutritional impact can be suggested. First, if household surveys are planned for a project, a nutritional status module can be added to them. Enumerators are given special training and equipment to take the anthropometric measurements, although the techniques are quite feasible for even junior staff. The two advantages of incorporating nutritional modules into household surveys are obvious: little extra cost is involved, and anthropometric variables can be analyzed with reference to relevant household variables. For example, farm size, type of food crops grown, or family size can be related to the nutritional status of the children in a household.

Figure 9. Output from Monthly Data Collected in Three Clinics by
the Consultories Senesores System in Santiago, Chile, 1977–80

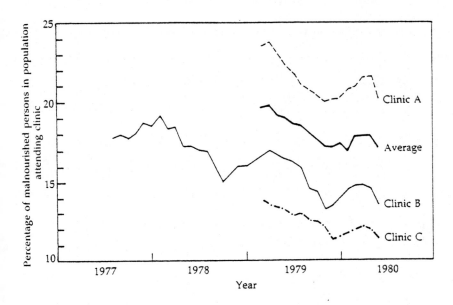

Source: J. Mason, J. Habricht, H. Tabatabai, and V. Valverde, *Nutritional Surveillance* (Geneva: World Health Organization, 1984). Used by permission.

Second, community weighing programs can be designed to indicate nutritional status by taking anthropometric measurements at specified intervals in selected areas. Indonesia and the Philippines have instituted national weighing programs under which the weights and heights of the children in selected provinces are recorded semiannually. Scaled-down community weighing programs can certainly be introduced in project areas. The sample size required will be substantial but, in view of the simplicity of the measurements, manageable.

Third, attempts can be made to record anthropometric data in village clinics and schools. Clinics can be persuaded to record routinely the weight of the children delivered and the weight and height of the children brought for treatment. Participating schools in the program can be provided with the necessary equipment. Financial or other inducements can be given to clinics and schools which effectively participate in the program. The generated data can be used with the caveat that the analysts recognize the biases introduced by inequities in the access to these facilities for different socioeconomic groups or populations from different areas. In many countries, such programs already exist.

Target Group Participation

Participation is rather difficult to define, but the underlying idea is deceptively simple. For target populations (or, more appropriately, a segment of them) to participate in an agriculture or rural development project simply means that they are involved directly in planning and implementing the principal development activities that affect them. In practice, of course, they are encouraged to make greater inputs during implementation than at the planning stage. Participation can take several forms, ranging from an advisory role as a representative of all the beneficiaries to responsibility for such activities as maintenance of the project's infrastructure.

Depending on their design and substantive focus, agriculture and rural development projects support the formation of different types of beneficiary organizations and provide technical and financial assistance to them. Reorganizing an existing grass-roots group or organization to facilitate its operations is simpler than creating such an organization. Many projects allocate resources for grass-roots beneficiary organizations, which are usually encouraged to perform one or more of the following functions:

- Disseminate information among the target populations about the project's objectives, activities, resources, time frame, and underlying approach to encourage them to take advantage of the opportunities

- Generate support for the project or a specific component that envisages radical changes in existing attitudes and behavior patterns (for example, water usage charges, resettlement of villagers affected by irrigation schemes, or changes in land tenure arrangements)

- Raise resources in cash or in kind for specific project activities (for example, donation of labor for the construction of roads or building schools)

- Distribute agricultural inputs among the target populations

- Disseminate technical advice among the target populations; in this category one may include contact farmers in the training and visit extension system who spread the messages provided by the extension agent to their neighbors and encourage their attendance during the scheduled visits of the extension agent

- Articulate the opinions, reactions, and interests of the target populations to appropriate authorities.

Farmers' clubs, water users' associations, village marketing societies, or small farmers' associations are some examples of beneficiary organizations.

The overall effects and impact of a project on beneficiary participation can be measured best by the emergence of viable organizations which demonstrate initiative and mobilize local resources for specific development endeavors. The evaluation of such organizations requires an in-depth study of both their existing and potential roles. Certain aspects of beneficiary organizations lend themselves to impact analysis:

- *The number and growth of beneficiary organizations.* The number of farmers' clubs or village cooperatives can run into hundreds depending, of course, on the size and the geographical coverage of the project. Relevant questions are: Is their number adequate to meet the requirements of the target populations? What proportions of the eligible target populations have joined them? What do the growth rates indicate for their evolution?

- *Organizational structure.* The success of the beneficiary organizations also depends on their organizational structures. Several questions need to be raised: How are the roles and responsibilities distributed? Is the structure conducive to open discussions? How are the decisions made? Do these organizations have the requisite authority and resources to undertake the functions expected of them?

- *Functions.* The critical questions include: Have beneficiary organizations been able to perform their functions effectively and efficiently? Are they capable of taking on new roles and responsibilities in the light of the changing project environment?

- *Leadership.* Participatory organizations can be dominated by elites whose interests are not always identical to those of the target populations that they are supposed to represent. For example, prosperous commercial farmers are usually able to control village credit institutions or cooperative marketing societies that were promoted to help the smallholders. Thus the pertinent questions are: What is the nature of the leadership? Is it truly representative of the target populations? What is its socioeconomic background?

- *Contribution to project effectiveness.* Questions include: Have the grass-roots organizations played a significant role in achieving the project objectives and raising understanding and critical consciousness among the target populations? Have the organizations demonstrated their ability to coordinate the target populations in certain servicing operations and in the maintenance of facilities?

- *Long-term viability.* The long-term viability of participatory organizations is critical. When the participatory organizations are kept alive only by the constant infusion of technical and financial resources from the project or other agencies, their very purpose is defeated. Under such situations, they do not engender self-reliance and initiative but foster a sense of dependency. Impact studies therefore should be able to answer such questions as: Have beneficiary organizations acquired, or are they acquiring, the necessary capabilities to sustain themselves? Is their reliance on outside funds increasing or decreasing? Have they developed a popular base of support which can be translated into greater leverage of the target populations in the political arena?

Example 29 summarizes a midterm evaluation of one type of beneficiary organization.

EXAMPLE 29. *Farmers' Clubs*

The midterm evaluation of an area development project in an East African country found that farmers' clubs had been largely responsible for increasing the demand and effectiveness of the credit component. As grass-roots institutions, originally promoted by extension agents to encourage the adoption of innovations, the clubs functioned as the main delivery system for credit to farmers. Two years after project start-up, farmers' clubs in the project area had expanded from 61 to 403 and had channeled credit to 12,800 members—about 33 percent of the area's farmers.

The evaluation team held meetings with club members to examine the reasons for the steady growth of the clubs and their increasing influence in the area. Farmers emphasized that they joined the clubs because credit resources were scarce and their membership helped them gain access to both seasonal loans and seasonal inputs. Extension advice also seemed to be more regular, and assistance was provided by members to each other in times of need.

The team also found that membership in the clubs had strengthened the farmers' commitment to the project. The clubs were well organized, with democratic constitutions and formal procedures. Meetings were held generally at least once a month, and some clubs even imposed fines for absences. Clubs decided how the credit would be distributed and also assumed collective responsibility to repay farmers' loans. An almost unparalleled record of close to 100 percent repayment was achieved—at least in part the result of the policy that denied a defaulting club further credit.

Source: IFAD.

Indicators

Examples of indicators to measure beneficiary participation are:

- Number of new organizations formed
- Number of organizations that existed before the project which received assistance for their reorganization or development

- Total membership of the beneficiary organizations
- Proportion of the adult target population that has joined these organizations or is serviced by them
- Proportion of the members who regularly attend the meetings of these organizations
- Status of self-financing in the organizations
- Volume of such inputs as improved seeds or credit distributed in a year, and its proportion of total input delivery
- Number of individuals who regularly received technical advice from beneficiary organizations
- Days of labor contributed by members to project activities
- Financial resources raised by members for specific tasks or activities of the project.

Data Collection Strategies

The data required to construct the above indicators generally can be gathered from the records and documents kept by the beneficiary organizations, project authorities, and governmental agencies. If no credible documentation is available, visits to these organizations can generate useful information. The absence of documentation and the degree of difficulty in estimating the missing numbers are themselves negative indicators of organizational performance. But more important than these indicators are the in-depth studies that should be undertaken on the wide range of topics identified above. In fact, in many instances conclusions drawn on the basis of indicators can be misleading in that they might fail to capture the underlying intricate, complex reality. Large membership figures can be deceptive if members cannot effectively participate in the organizations or do not attend their meetings. The data on loan disbursements can give us a misleading picture if village credit societies are unable to recover them. Moreover, the inner dynamics of these organizations cannot be assessed only on the basis of simplistic indicators.

The required qualitative studies should be designed carefully and planned using one or more of a wide variety of such methods as participant observation, qualitative interviews, informal surveys, or group meetings with a cross-section of the members and the leaders of these organizations. Such investigations will be able to provide descriptive, detailed information, interpretations, and recommendations grounded in empirical experience. These studies are similar to the problem diagnostic studies discussed in chapter 5.

The concept of participation leads logically to the recommendation that members and leaders of the beneficiary organizations should whenever possible be involved in collecting, analyzing, and interpreting the evaluation data. Their participation can add an insider's perspective to that of the outside evaluators while alerting the beneficiary organizations to the sponsoring agencies' perceptions of their roles, achievements, and failures. The inclusion of beneficiaries is often expressed in the evaluation design more as a pious avowal of good intentions than as a concrete part. It is true that encouraging self-evaluation is not easy, but in certain circumstances an effort to bring this about can be most rewarding for the project's evaluators as well as its participants.

The Status and Role of Women

The analysis of the impact of agricultural and rural development projects on women farmers has changed over time. In the past, the primary concern was with equity; evaluations attempted to determine if women farmers benefited from the intervention to the same extent, if not in the same fashion, as male farmers. This concern paved the way for a more integrated recognition that the issue is not merely one of equity but also one of balanced development. Agriculture cannot advance without effectively mobilizing the efforts and resources of the women who play a critical role in it. Thus the impact should be analyzed within the wider context of the participation of women in agriculture.

Women's participation in agricultural tasks forms four patterns:

- *Responsibility for specific crops.* Women and men often produce and sell different crops and products. For example, women may grow subsistence crops and men cash crops. Or women may engage in horticulture and men in the cultivation of cereals. In many parts of Africa, men tend cattle and women small stock.

- *Separate fields.* Women may produce the same crops as men but on different fields. They usually grow crops for domestic consumption. A good example is the agricultural system in West Africa: each wife cultivates her own plot in addition to the fields owned by her husband or the extended family. In such systems, a woman is responsible primarily for all agricultural operations and inputs on her own fields.

- *Separate tasks.* Agricultural tasks are often distributed on the basis of gender. For example, men prepare the ground, plow it, and transport the produce, while women plant, weed, and do any necessary storage and processing. Women take care of trees, but harvesting, which might require climbing, is done by men.

- *Female holders.* Many farms (holdings) are run fully by women because the senior male members of the family are absent as a result of death, divorce, or short- and long-term migration to nearby towns or cities in search of a better means of livelihood.

These patterns of women's participation should be kept in view when analyzing the impact of development interventions that affect the production roles, employment, incomes, and social status of women and the intrahousehold allocation of resources. Obviously, not all the influences of a project on these dimensions can be examined in each individual impact evaluation. There are constraints of time and resources. Moreover, the cultural and social sensibilities of the local populations should not be overlooked. It is often prudent to focus on a few topics which can be studied in depth rather than to examine a wide range of subjects superficially. We mention here a few areas which might be considered for impact analysis.

Access to Project Inputs and Services

One simple strategy to assess the impact of a project on women farmers is to determine the extent to which they received their fair share of its inputs and services. To give a simple example, if 30 percent of the credit in a project went to women farmers and their percentage of the total farming population is about the same, we can conclude that they received a reasonable share. But if only 10 percent of the amount was distributed among women farmers, reservations can be raised about the accessibility of the credit to women. To study access, we can consider one or more of the following items: agricultural inputs such as seeds or fertilizers, extension advice, training or educational programs, and beneficiary organizations formed by the project.

Unless conscious efforts are made during the design and implementation stages, women farmers are not likely to get their fair share. This happens not necessarily because of any conscious neglect by the project personnel but primarily because of the cultural, social, and economic barriers faced by women. Discrimination in access to project inputs and facilities reflects the institutionalized discrimination that exists in a society against women. Some explanatory variables for the low accessibility are:

- Lack of legal ownership of land, livestock, or other assets which can be used as surety or as a proof of their farming activities
- Domestic responsibilities which limit women's participation in extension advice or training programs
- Cultural barriers in the society which prohibit free interactions between persons of opposite sex, particularly when they belong to different communities; under such conditions, women farmers are not able to converse with male extension workers, medical personnel, or government officials (see example 30)
- Low social and cultural status, which leads to underrepresentation in

beneficiary organizations and places women in a disadvantageous position when inputs and services are provided through such organizations

- Illiteracy and lack of education, which are likely to be proportionately greater for women than men.

EXAMPLE 30. *Cultural Barriers between Male Officials and Women Farmers*

A project in Asia focused on distributing improved breeds of poultry and giving extension advice on their care. But before the improved breeds could be distributed, a massive poultry vaccination campaign had to be launched in villages to eliminate sources of disease which could wipe out the new breeds.

The traditional practice was for a livestock assistant to make the rounds of each village every three months to vaccinate the poultry. But poultry kept by village women was being missed under this practice because the women were in purdah and it was considered culturally inappropriate for male livestock assistants to visit the women's homes to vaccinate their poultry if their husbands were not present. A large portion of the men usually worked outside the village, and if the poultry was missed during the first visit, the livestock assistant's busy schedule often did not permit him to return.

The women's unvaccinated poultry was a potential source of disease; therefore, the introduction of improved breeds had to be delayed until the entire village's flock had been vaccinated. Because the success of the project strategy as a whole depended on reaching village women, the project director had women trained as livestock assistants.

Source: FAO.

If male and female farmers are raising different crops or are engaged in different agricultural operations, they certainly do not require the same inputs and services. For instance, if men grow wheat, which is regarded as a cash crop and a male preserve, and the input and service package promoted by the project focuses on this, it would be a mistake to expect women farmers to be able to use the project package. Under such conditions, the comparison between male and female farmers would be misleading. An important issue, however, whether the project also provided inputs that were relevant to the needs of women farmers. This is, of course, an altogether different matter.

The data on the access to inputs and services can be easily gathered by perusing project records and documents and by conducting formal or informal surveys if necessary. For projects with a beneficiary contact monitoring system, such data will be collected regularly, and necessary corrective steps will be taken if problems of access emerge.

Employment and Workload

The overall employment effects of a project are generally considered in evaluations and do not require elaboration. But the effects of a project on the workload of women farmers are usually overlooked. In addition to being farmers and producers, women shoulder such considerable domestic responsibilities as cooking, cleaning, fetching water, gathering wood for fuel, and child bearing and rearing. They must do these chores whether they are involved in agricultural operations or not. Therefore additional production activities promoted by the project add to their already heavy workload. For example, in some projects the introduction of two cropping seasons made possible by an improved variety of wheat seed virtually doubled the workload of women farmers. The additional workload often became a large impediment to the adoption of agricultural innovations and thus adversely affected the implementation of the projects. In a project in Thailand, the increase in work led families to drop out of farm trials. In a Caribbean project, women exerted pressure on their husbands to stop growing bananas for the same reason. Agricultural innovations or development activities can also reduce the workload of women. The provision of potable water has reduced the time spent by women on procuring water. Mechanized rice milling has undoubtedly relieved many women of a heavy work burden.

Studies are needed on the effect of project interventions on the employment patterns and workload of women. These studies could use the qualitative and quantitative data generated by key informants, informal interviews with women farmers, and formal sample surveys if necessary. Variables to include in the studies are: inventory of the tasks performed; nature of the tasks; variability of the tasks in time required and frequency of occurrence; characteristics of the individual performing the tasks; time burden on various household members; and the process and rationale for task allocation.

Intrahousehold Allocation of Resources

In recent years there has been a growing emphasis on the intrahousehold allocation of resources, which stems from the recognition that although the household remains the primary unit for production and consumption in subsistence economies all its adult members do not have equal access to its resources or enjoy equal decisionmaking power. Moreover, although the members have a shared interest, they also have individual interests which might not be mutually compatible. As a result, household resources are not always consumed or invested with reference to the needs and interests of all its members. The differences in the power and authority of the members affect the allocation process. And since in most societies male members enjoy greater authority and power, women farmers might not get their fair share of the incomes from and resources of development. Therefore it has been suggested that evaluations should also focus on the intrahousehold allocation of resources in terms of domestic consumption as well as agricultural activities.

Qualitative anthropological studies are the most economical way to understand how resources are allocated among target populations. These studies should focus on the decisionmaking authority of the various members of the household in terms of both production and expenditure. To conduct expenditure and consumption surveys to probe intrahousehold variations is scarcely feasible as a part of the evaluation of a project.

The Environment

How to intensify agriculture while balancing the demands on the natural resource base and avoiding adverse environmental consequences has become a central question in assuring project effectiveness. As experience has shown, the range of possible environmental consequences of a project is wide given the complex and often subtle nature of ecological systems and linkages. The discussion that follows therefore can only serve to introduce the topic in order to highlight its importance and illustrate the need to measure impacts of projects on the natural resource base in terms of their direct, indirect, and cumulative effects. Some of the resource management issues commonly associated with agriculture projects are:

- Maintaining soil productivity (for example, erosion control, land preparation, and harvesting techniques)
- Water resource management (for example, pollution, salinization, and sedimentation)
- Land use management (for example, conversion of critical natural areas to other uses, land settlement patterns, area devoted to food crops and cash crops, and wildlife habitats)
- Fertilizer and pesticide application (contamination of soils and water, human health problems, and disturbance of natural crop-predator balances)
- Assurance of human livelihood (access to natural resources, involuntary resettlement, and protection of vulnerable ethnic minorities)
- Incidence of environmentally related disease (spread of disease, creation of new vector habitats, and methods of control).

At the project design stage the potential impact of the planned activities is identified and the risks are weighed. Special consideration should be given to the new socioeconomic and environmental conditions to be produced. On existing farmland, for example, the mix of new crops proposed by a project can influence farming practices or food self-sufficiency. In addition, it can increase the susceptibility of crops to pest attacks, droughts, or other environmental hazards. Attention should not be confined to land under cultivation, but should extend to surrounding watersheds, wetlands, and other natural areas. The management of these unique resources is within the scope of project activities, for they are often critical to the sustainability of agriculture as well as to local populations that may depend heavily on them for water, fuel, food, and timber; see example 31.

Data collection will of course differ with the type of project and the complexity of its potential impact on the natural resource base. Some projects include components specifically designed to examine the consequences of project activities. Natural resource inventories or ecological research are two examples. The physical changes in the project area may be recorded through such techniques as remote sensing, for example, to assess forest resources or to monitor changes in land use patterns. Data collection may also involve periodic sampling, such as chemical analysis of water and soils to monitor for critical levels of pesticides or biological activity. Surveys can also be used to gain information on local perceptions of the project's influence on natural resource use and especially to assess farmer support for conservation practices.

EXAMPLE 31. Inadequate Attention to Environmental Considerations

The following two projects present situations in which natural resource issues were superficially addressed at appraisal and inadequately incorporated into the design of the projects. The impacts of these projects extended well beyond the project areas and caused economically and ecologically costly problems which required special studies to identify solutions.

In an irrigation project, the excessive, uncoordinated and indiscriminate use of insecticides produced serious problems in the project area. Farmers tended to apply any chemical they were able to purchase because of market shortages and to spray too often and at the wrong time. Project staff were unable to identify many of the chemicals and enforce an appropriate regime of application. This had adverse impacts on crop production since many of the pests began to develop a resistance to the chemicals and many of their natural predators had been wiped out.

The master plan for a land settlement project noted that wildlife sanctuaries would be needed where land was cleared. But no precise action was proposed at appraisal. During implementation it became evident that severe competition for land had developed between settlers and wildlife. Losses of crops, delays in settlers' entry, and animal control measures all contributed to the project's high cost overrun. Indiscriminate clearing of land also threat-

ened the habitat of locally important flora and fauna. At project completion, it was all too evident that preventive measures had been warranted and that special provision for wildlife protection should have been included as project components.

Source: World Bank.

For data needs to be assessed competently at the outset of a project, at least three points should be considered. First, the technical capability of the staff or access to trained personnel will affect the degree to which managers can evaluate changes in the natural resource base. When staff lack technical expertise, the information collected by various indicators tends merely to record change and to provide little understanding of the importance of change to project activities.

Second, the time frame allowed for data collection activities must also be considered. In general, the relatively short five- or six-year life of most projects makes it difficult to detect the slowly evolving changes in the natural resource base. For example, accurate estimates of soil loss in watersheds generally require a lengthy time series of measurements to detect the trend underlying random annual fluctuations caused by variations in rainfall. Data collection may have to be limited to indicators which in many instances are less accurate but more timely.

Third, it has been stressed throughout this book that although comprehensive monitoring may provide many of the data required for evaluation, in many cases additional information will be needed—particularly when unexpected, adverse environmental changes are encountered. When these unintended developments occur, existing data may not be adequate to enable project managers to isolate various factors and to establish causal relationships that were not previously identified. The monitoring and evaluation staff of a project must be alert to emerging environmental conditions that require specialized assistance, which in many situations must come from national or regional agencies.

In such circumstances, in-depth technical studies will be needed to determine the nature of the problems and to assess their seriousness. Normally, a project's resources for evaluation will not be sufficient for such studies, which require specialized skills and access to sophisticated equipment. Questions regarding pollution, for example, may require access to laboratory facilities and technicians. The study of possible human health consequences obviously requires the use of qualified medical researchers.

The Role of National Survey Agencies

Impact studies for at least some of the topics mentioned in this chapter—particularly standards of living and the environment—may require surveys of a scale, complexity, and duration beyond the scope of the data collection programs that can be expected from a project's monitoring and evaluation staff. A linkage is required between project evaluation systems and national survey capabilities. A longitudinal study required to assess social and economic change can be handled only by a national body responsible for surveys and data analysis, such as a national statistics office or an economics planning division in a ministry of agriculture. Such bodies can maintain a survey beyond the funding period of a specific project. They also have, or should have, the core of professional staff required for such an enterprise. Whether such a study is to be a priority for such a body is a matter for discussion between the relevant national authorities and potential users of the evaluation data. It is sometimes said of national statistical agencies that their program is not sufficiently responsive to the requirements of their potential clientele. At some level of the national debate, it is necessary to consider an integrated program of rural data collection and analysis that assigns appropriate roles to organizations ranging from a national statistics office to a project monitoring and evaluation unit.

To build an executing agency's capability to monitor activities is of course an important institutional objective. But the resources to conduct a number of complex, large-scale surveys cannot be made available to each sector or lending agency. If there is no national capability to handle such surveys, a surrogate for one should not be constructed just to deal with the longitudinal data requirements of a single development project or even program. Either more modest ambitions must be agreed upon pending the development of a national survey capacity, or assistance must be provided immediately to accelerate the development of such a capacity within the plan for the country's statistical services.

Suggested Readings

Byerlee, Derek, Michael Collinson, and International Maize and Wheat Improvement Center. *Planning Technologies Appropriate to Farmers: Concepts and Procedures*. Mexico City: International Maize and Wheat Improvement Center, 1980.

Casley, Dennis J., and Denis A. Lury. *Data Collection in Developing Countries*. London: Oxford University Press, 1981.

————. *Monitoring and Evaluation of Agriculture and Rural Development Projects*. Baltimore, Md.: Johns Hopkins University Press, 1981.

Cernea, Michael. *Measuring Project Impact: Monitoring and Evaluation in the PIDER Rural Development Project—Mexico*. World Bank Staff Working Paper 332. Washington, D.C., 1979.

Cernea, Michael, and Benjamin Tepping. *A System of Monitoring and Evaluating Agricultural Extension Projects*. World Bank Staff Working Paper 272. Washington, D.C., 1977.

Chambers, Robert. *Managing Rural Development: Ideas and Experience from East Africa*. Uppsala, Sweden: Scandinavian Institute of African Studies, 1974.

————. *Rural Development: Putting the Last First*. London: Longman, 1983.

Chander, Ramesh, Christiaan Grootaert, and Graham Pyatt. *Living Standards Surveys in Developing Countries*. Living Standards Measurement Study Working Paper 1. Washington, D.C.: World Bank, 1985.

Clayton, Eric, and Françoise Petry. *Monitoring Systems for Agricultural and Rural Development Projects*. Vol. 1. FAO Economic and Social Development Paper 12, rev. 1. Rome, 1983.

Conant, Francis, Peter Rogers, Marion Baumgardner, Cyrus McKell, Raymond Dasmann, and P. Reining. Eds. *Resource Inventory and Baseline Study Methods for Developing Countries*. Washington, D.C.: American Association for the Advancement of Science, 1983.

FAO. *Estimation of Crop Areas and Yields in Agricultural Statistics*. FAO Economic and Social Development Paper 22. Rome, 1982.

Gittinger, J. Price. *The Economic Analysis of Agricultural Projects*. Baltimore, Md.: Johns Hopkins University Press, 1982.

Hansen, Morris, William N. Hurwitz, and William G. Madow. *Sample Survey Methods and Theory*. New York: Wiley, 1953.

Hoaglin, David, Frederick Mosteller, and John W. Tukey. Eds. *Exploring Data Tables, Trends, and Shapes.* London: Wiley, 1985.

Kish, Leslie. *Survey Sampling.* London: Wiley, 1965.

Lee, James A. *The Environment, Public Health, and Human Ecology: Considerations for Economic Development.* Baltimore, Md.: Johns Hopkins University Press, 1985.

Mason, John, J. Habicht, H. Tabatabai, and V. Valverde. *Nutritional Surveillance.* Geneva: World Health Organization, 1984.

Miles, Matthew, and A. Michael Huberman. *Qualitative Data Analysis: A Sourcebook of New Methods.* Beverly Hills, Calif.: Sage, 1984.

Mulvaney, John E. *Analysis Bar Charting.* Washington, D.C.: World Bank, 1975.

Murphy, J., and L. Sprey. *Introduction to Farm Surveys.* Wageningen, The Netherlands: International Institute for Land Reclamation and Improvement, 1983.

————. *Monitoring and Evaluation of Agricultural Change.* Wageningen, The Netherlands: International Institute for Land Reclamation and Improvement, 1982.

Ng., Ronald, and Francis Lethem. *Monitoring Systems and Irrigation Management: An Experience from the Philippines.* Washington, D.C.: World Bank, 1983.

Patton, Michael R. *Utilization-Focused Evaluation.* Beverly Hills, Calif.: Sage, 1986.

Poate, C. D., and Dennis J. Casley. *Estimating Crop Production in Development Projects: Methods and their Limitations.* Washington, D.C.: World Bank, 1985.

Rossi, Peter H., and Howard E. Freeman. *Evaluation: A Systematic Approach.* Beverly Hills, Calif.: Sage, 1985.

Scott, Chris. *Sampling for Monitoring and Evaluation.* Washington, D.C.: World Bank, 1985.

Smith, Peter. *Agricultural Project Management: Monitoring and Control of Implementation.* London: Elsevier, 1984.

U.N. ACC Task Force on Rural Development. *Guiding Principles for the Design and Use of Monitoring and Evaluation in Rural Development Projects and Programs.* Rome, 1984.

UNICEF and World Food Program. *Food Aid and the Well-Being for Children in the Developing World.* New York: UNICEF, 1986.

Index